FROM NIGHT TO LIGHT

My Brain Injury Journey from Despair to Hope, Faith, and Joy

D0839653

DONNA JONES

ISBN 978-1-64114-592-3 (Paperback)
ISBN 978-1-64114-593-0 (Digital)

Christian Faith Publishing, Inc.
296 Chestnut Street
Meadville, PA 16335
www.christianfaithpublishing.com

Printed in the United States of America

This book is dedicated
to brain injury survivors
and their families.

CONTENTS

FOREWORD

Dear reader,

"Donna Jones" was a name that my coworkers often mentioned and eventually recommended when I was looking for a motivated, energetic, positive, hardworking candidate for a job that I needed filled in my organization back in 2005. Her name was somewhat iconic and referred to more like a commodity than a person, similar to the Pillsbury Dough Boy, the Energizer Bunny, Mr. Clean, or the Geico lizard from the insurance commercials. She was "branded" and well known.

After I met Donna, I had a better understanding of why she had such a lasting "aura" and left such a positive impression wherever she went. Her positive attitude, her genuine kindness and willingness to help others unconditionally was why she made such an impact and the reason why others commoditized the "Donna Jones" name. Of course, Donna had no idea this phenomenon was going on around her, and if she did, I can assure you it would have made her blush.

Needless to say, I hired Donna on my team, and we had a positive professional relationship for a couple years until I left the company. Afterward, she and I continued to stay in touch and developed a deep friendship that continues today, eight years later. My family knows her well. They love her very much and feel a special bond with her. My husband and I were honored a few years ago when she agreed to give the blessing at our wedding in front of our friends and family. She looked radiant that day and truly glowed like an angel. She really did! My daughters and nieces affectionately call her "Miss Donna." She is considered part of my family and extended family.

One of Donna's greatest gifts is her faith in God and her gentle and subtle teaching of her beliefs and how each one of us can benefit from them every day. She lives her life by living by example as a true disciple of God. After her brain injury many years ago, Donna had many ups and downs and challenges to overcome. She used her faith in God to give her the strength to get through those difficult times. During my friendship with Donna, she was healed of her brain injury through God's love, grace, and presence inside her.

In my own life, when making life-changing decisions, Donna's friendship, support, and love during this time helped make my transition easier and helped me stay positive and strong for my family.

Over the years, I have joined Donna at several brain injury events where she shares her personal story with others, either in a private one-on-one conversation or at the podium during speaking sessions in front of large audiences. The people she talks to all have different issues and challenges, but what always amazes me is the impact she has on them. Her own testimonial on how she overcame her brain injury is inspiring and her positive energy contagious. It is amazing to watch the "aura" of Donna Jones and how she influences others to thrive.

I am Donna's friend, and I love her for all the goodness she shares with me and my family, brain injury and all.

Dawn

PREFACE

As a brain injury survivor, I realized how alone I felt on this journey, even with the doctors and people I would meet along the way. Everywhere I went, no one had heard about a brain injury, and no one knew how to handle what I was experiencing. Friends didn't want to hang around and wait for my symptoms to disappear while others weren't sure if I could handle being out and about and away from home. As the years as a survivor continued, I became determined to share my story as well as teach anyone who would listen what it was like to live with this disability.

The more people I met, the more determined I became to educate everyone on the symptoms as well as share the incredible numbers of people in the world living with this devastating disability. I would learn there are more people living with this disability than any other disease or disability combined, yet it seemed to be a silent disability.

When I shared my story with friends or even people on the street, almost everyone would immediately say, "You should write a book." I would typically smile and make an excuse. I didn't feel I had a story to tell and couldn't imagine anyone being interested in reading about it. The brain injury survivors I met along my journey seemed so much worse off than me as my story began with a little bump on my head while others were in comas or needing full-time care.

Well, here I am writing my story and praying someone who picks this up will benefit and be blessed by my journey. As a survivor, you get to learn so much about yourself and how much you can

FROM NIGHT TO LIGHT

handle as well as what it takes to begin a new life in what feels like a strange new body and brain.

There are so many people to thank for not only making this book possible but for helping and guiding me through this incredible journey. My friends/coworkers helped me for many years while I tried to come back to the office and pick up the pieces of my life. I hope they get to read this book and realize what a huge impact they were in my journey. Thanks to people in my life now who have encouraged me to write this book and how much they help and encourage me each and every day.

Thanks to my initial editors, Marlene, Margaret, and Karen, for helping me to put words that made sense on paper. To Janis, who took my first manuscript and showed me how to format it into a book and how to tighten up my words, thanks for teaching me how to eliminate the extra words and link sentences together.

And finally, to Adrienne, who took time away from her family to be my final editor and proofreader. She also helped me fill in the areas of my journey where I hadn't provided enough detail as well as encouraged me to publish my story.

INTRODUCTION

On Friday, January 6, 1995, a traumatic brain injury from a car accident altered my world forever. Before that day, if someone had said I wouldn't be able to do something or that a job was too big for me to handle, I would not have believed them. With determination, I always succeeded—I almost felt invincible. But after the accident, everything changed. My confident and successful work life suddenly became complicated and overwhelming. I couldn't understand what people were saying to me or remember the names of coworkers I had known for years. Confused and trapped inside my head, it even seemed difficult to walk and breathe.

What did the doctors tell me? They explained that I would no longer be able to hold down a full-time job. I wouldn't be capable of learning anything new. I couldn't ski down my favorite mountain. I couldn't participate in mainstream society like before. In short, there was no way I would be able to live the life I had prior to the accident.

Well, I'm going to tell you how I beat the odds.

1

Life before the Brain Injury

I never considered myself a workaholic or a Type A personality, but, in retrospect, I was a classic example of both. I had a great career at AT&T and was completing my bachelor's degree in business administration at Seton Hall University. I worked full-time days as well as taking three evening courses with a grade point average close to 4.0.

I had a tremendous amount of energy and many times was compared to the Energizer Bunny—I kept going and going and going, never stopping, always needing to be busy. In addition to work and school, my spare time consisted of studying, going to the movies, skiing, league bowling, playing softball, going to parties, attending Broadway shows and local plays, taking weekend trips, working with the Special Olympics, and much, much more.

I quickly climbed the corporate ladder at AT&T. Starting in the mailroom, I was promoted to advancing levels about every six months and worked my way up to a manager's level in the Corporate Healthcare Department. As my responsibilities grew, so did my confidence and thirst to tackle more. My span of control steadily increased; there wasn't anything I felt I couldn't handle.

At school, I needed to excel and get an A in every course. Often, I assumed the leadership role in each class, and many times teachers would use my work experience to help teach the class. I enjoyed learning as well as helping others learn. I assisted students during and after class, meeting with them in the library and spending late nights to coach them in calculus. I made myself available to my fellow students an hour before each class period to help them cram for a test or just review the previous day's lessons; no request for help was denied.

I had a very active social life and really enjoyed being around people. On the job, whenever new coworkers joined my organization, I was the first person to greet them and make them feel at ease. It seemed to come natural to me. I organized parties at home and work, always thinking up different types of events that would be fun for everyone. I created themes for our bowling league, such as Halloween night, the 50's, the Olympics, etc., always thinking about new ideas. My brain never stopped; there was always something new to create. At work, I pulled together softball and bowling tournaments between organizations. I was the go-to girl. If someone needed a creative idea or just something fun to do, I was the person they would come to. I loved it! It felt like I was on the go 24 hours a day. I didn't need to eat or sleep. I just kept going and going and going. I was indestructible. Nothing could bring me down—or so I thought.

THE ACCIDENT

I will never forget Friday, January 6, 1995. The first week in January was extremely busy and stressful for many of us at work, and I was no exception. We were working on a new benefit program, and I was obsessed with making sure everything was perfect before leaving for the weekend. That night, instead of leaving work on time to go to a surprise baby shower with my coworkers, I stayed to finish a couple of things. For a workaholic, there was always something to finish up or continue to work on. I just didn't know how to quit.

I didn't realize there was a snowstorm brewing outside until I left the office and noticed it was snowing and there was a small accumulation on the road. I expected the roads might be slippery so was very careful driving, although I was never afraid to drive in the snow and felt very comfortable behind the wheel.

As I approached the house where the baby shower was being held, the snow seemed to have stopped and disappeared from the streets. What I didn't realize was that the road was covered with black ice and in only a few seconds, my car was about to spin out of control and change my entire life. Even though the roads now appeared safe, I still took precaution and slowly made a left-hand turn. Immediately after and without warning, I must have lost traction, and my front left tire hit the guardrail, thus spinning my car off the road and into the woods. Even with wearing my seat belt, I somehow hit my head on what I believe was the side panel frame just above the window. I don't know if I lost consciousness or not. It didn't feel like I did, but I am not 100 percent sure. I vaguely remember someone in a red truck, although I was not positive since it was around 8:00 p.m. and darkness had already started to settle in. I remember a shadowy figure of a man approached my car window, coming to my aid. I don't ever recall seeing his face as he appeared in the dark, and it felt like out of the blue he approached my car. He asked me if I was all right, and I felt perfectly safe opening my door and allowing him to get into my car. This is totally out of character for me, and I didn't even hesitate to hand over my car, leaving my purse and belongings behind—God was definitely watching out for me and protecting me. I don't know if handing my car over to this man was because of the injury to my head or if I felt he may be a guardian angel coming to my aid. Once in my car, he somehow managed to maneuver my car out of the woods and back on the road again. The good news is that the accident happened near my home and I only had to drive my car a short distance. Since I was shaken up quite a bit, I decided to go straight home instead of continuing on to the baby shower.

At home safe and sound, I tried to stay awake for a while just in case I had a concussion, but I was so tired and fell asleep sitting upright in my living room chair.

To my amazement, I woke up the next day still sitting in my recliner chair and feeling fine. I did not stop to think something could be wrong; instead I proceeded in my normal organized and Energizer Bunny fashion and began to tackle the first task on my agenda to get my car fixed. I called AAA, and someone came to assess the damages to my car. The mechanic told me that my car was not drivable and was shocked when I told him I had driven it from the scene of the accident.

My car was towed away, and later in the week, I found out that there was $8,000 worth of damage to the gears and driving mechanisms, which would make it impossible to steer or drive. My car looked perfectly fine on the outside, and so did I—neither of us had a scratch on us—but internally the car was a disaster, and soon I would find out that I had sustained a serious injury to my brain.

I spent most of the weekend after the accident sleeping, feeling extremely tired and really out of it. At the time, I thought it was because of the hectic week I experienced prior to the accident, but now know it was because of the injury to my brain.

On Monday morning, I arose ready to begin a new week. What I didn't know was that I was about to begin a whole new journey.

As I tried to get ready for work, I felt disoriented and very dizzy. I can only describe it as a spinning sensation inside my body without my body moving. The closest comparison is what is referred to as "sea legs" when cruising but a much worst case. I remember feeling very strange inside and unable to explain what was going on. I called my coworker who was going to drive me to work. Lucky for me, she was a nurse. I explained my symptoms to her, and she immediately told me to go to the hospital. Unfortunately, she was unable to take me herself due to an early meeting she needed to attend at her job. She suggested I call a taxi to take me to the hospital. I should have begun to realize yet another clue that something was wrong when I couldn't figure out how to call for a taxi. I remember asking her, "How do I find a taxi?" Her response was to use the yellow pages, which I followed up with, "Where can I find the yellow pages?" Yes, we actually had a physical book of phone numbers, and the cover of the book was yellow.

She ended up calling a taxi for me, and I was soon on my way to the hospital. I remember how challenging it was just walking down the stairs of my condo and trying to figure out how to pay for the taxi. I felt like I was in a fog or having an out-of-body experience. Things were very confusing and not making any sense.

At the hospital, the doctor indicated I had a concussion and I would be fine. No x-rays or any other tests were taken. He just looked into my eyes to determine his diagnosis. He prescribed codeine for pain, even though I had no pain, and was released from the hospital. The doctor said I could return to work the next day as long as I wasn't taking the codeine, as it would make me very drowsy and difficult to focus. That worked for me! I didn't have any pain, so I certainly didn't feel I needed to take the codeine. I was ready and able to go back to work—or so I thought. I felt silly that I had even made the trip to the hospital. I considered myself indestructible. Nothing could keep me down. I was now determined to prove to everyone that there was nothing wrong with me.

I don't remember calling into work sick on Monday before going to the hospital, but after returning home, I called my boss to explain what had happened and what the doctor determined. As a precaution, my boss insisted I take the week off. I thought it was a little excessive but also thought that after working nonstop for several weeks, it would be a great opportunity to have a week to myself to enjoy a little fun and relaxation. Little did I know that my expectations would be crushed because as each day progressed, my symptoms steadily worsened.

I returned to work the next week, and as the days and weeks progressed, I became more and more confused, disoriented, and progressively feeling trapped inside my body. All the while I kept trying to show everyone there was nothing wrong with me. But there definitely was something wrong. I had no idea how to sort out what was happening.

Finally, my friend and coworker—the nurse I mentioned earlier—suggested I see a neurologist. I agreed. But would I be able to explain well enough what was happening to me? Would they take me seriously? Would someone be able to stop the spinning inside of me?

Would I finally be able to understand why I couldn't recognize some of my coworkers or answer simple questions?

THE CHALLENGE OF GETTING SOMEONE TO LISTEN

Getting doctors to listen is one of the greatest challenges facing a brain injury survivor. My experience was that unless you are lying in a hospital bed unconscious, it is unlikely many doctors will listen to you or take you seriously.

The first neurologist saw me for a few minutes once a week. She would sit across the room and ask me how the week went. I would explain how I spent most of my time sleeping and that when I was awake, I had pain shooting through my head. I told her how dizzy and disoriented I felt and that when people spoke, I didn't understand what they were saying. I told her that sitting in a meeting at work was overwhelming, and I had trouble paying attention. I knew people were talking, but had no idea what they were saying. My head was foggy and cloudy all the time, and I also felt like I had the worst case of the flu I'd ever had in my entire life.

The neurologist would listen, nod her head, and write notes, barely even looking up at me. Her response after hearing everything I said was to write me a prescription for medication. Each week I would go away with a new prescription to try. In her notes, she kept writing that I was "experiencing headaches." I tried to explain to her that there was a difference between a headache and shooting pain, but she wouldn't listen. This went on for several months.

In a 10-month period, I saw three different neurologists and several other general doctors before one doctor finally diagnosed me with a traumatic brain injury. He was truly amazed that no one listened to me since I was, in his words, very articulate explaining what was wrong with me. I came to him with a detailed list of symptoms and experiences I had kept track of since the very first symptom. He thought I had memorized a book on brain injuries as it practically matched a document of his that he showed me. It was amazing.

During this time, I began taking biofeedback sessions that were recommended to me by the first neurologist. She had a nurse in the office who administered them. I believe the exercises really did work. They helped me to stay calm and enabled me to manage the pain. Today, I still use some of the techniques I learned. Biofeedback is even great for anyone who is experiencing a lot of stress, especially for those, like myself, who are type A personalities.

Biofeedback exercises enabled me to take the pressure off my brain. When someone breaks an arm or a leg, the treatment is a cast and resting the broken bone for a period of time. So, how do you manage to rest your brain? Your brain controls everything—breathing, movement of all your extremities, eating, sleeping, etc. Your brain never shuts off, or at least mine never did. The challenge for me, as a workaholic with a type A personality, was to stop thinking for a period of time and rest my brain.

The nurse said that she thought I would have a very hard time with these exercises because I'm such an intense and focused individual. It was a good thing for me I was also a perfectionist. It made me want to prove her wrong by mastering the techniques. Not sure I did, but biofeedback did give me some relief and enabled me to slow down my brain activity so that it caused less pressure on my brain. In one of the following chapters, I will discuss biofeedback therapy in more detail.

After several months of struggling with my symptoms and having no real answers to what was happening, my friends decided it was time for me to see another doctor. Although I had positive results with the biofeedback exercises, the doctor seemed to only want to keep me medicated. She couldn't give me any answers except that I should wait because "these things" take time. What things? Why couldn't I function at work? Why was I in a fog? Why did I continually feel completely out of it? I needed answers to these questions, not someone who would just sit and arbitrarily take notes. I needed someone who would really listen to me.

So I ventured out to find another neurologist. Unfortunately, this one was arrogant and didn't seem to hear anything I said. Since I was sleeping so much and less active, my body started to slow down. I was having trouble breathing, walking, and moving my arms and legs. When I mentioned this to the new doctor, his question was "What do you think is wrong?" I wanted to reply, "Well, I guess if I knew what was wrong, I wouldn't be coming to see you!" He walked out of the office leaving me there upset and confused and returned with a prescription for Prozac. What was his diagnosis? I was depressed from the accident. Well, anyone who knew me could easily see that I wasn't depressed and that I was handling my troubling symptoms very well, although I think I was too out of it to really know what was happening to me. I remember sitting in my car so upset as to how this doctor treated me, like I was an emotional, depressed woman who needed to be further medicated, not a person who clearly hit her head and was struggling to find answers. It's devastating and hard enough for your brain and body to lose its ability to work normally, let alone be treated with so little respect.

Before filling the prescription for Prozac, I needed to have a blood test done by my primary care physician. He was convinced that I didn't need to take Prozac and was determined to find out through a blood test what was really happening to me. The test revealed that I was anemic and that my body was having trouble keeping the iron vitamin in my bloodstream. I began taking iron pills. This helped a little, but there was still something seriously wrong, and no one could figure it out.

During this time, my cousin who worked in the payroll office of a hospital overheard a person speaking about similar symptoms to what I was experiencing. She found out the name of the doctor treating that person. As fate would have it, this doctor happened to be visiting the hospital. Within a week, my cousin met with the doctor and explained my symptoms.

The doctor told my cousin that he would be willing to see me as a patient and try to help me. Since his office was several hours away from where I lived, my cousin said I could live with her, if necessary. However, as only God can orchestrate, this doctor had a college roommate with a similar practice who had an office a couple of miles away from my home and made arrangements for me to meet with him.

Finally, a doctor who would listen!

2

Living with a Brain Injury

I met with the doctor's college roommate. After speaking with him for a few minutes, he asked me what books I had read relating to brain injuries. I told him I hadn't read any and that I had never heard anything about brain injuries before. He said I seemed very knowledgeable about the symptoms, almost like I was reading from a book. At this time, I still believed I was dealing with a concussion. I never connected a concussion to a brain injury.

He expressed how articulate I was in relating what I had experienced and was shocked that not one of the other doctors picked up on what I described. He put me through a couple of neuropsychological-cognitive tests that I failed. I think this was the first time in my life I had actually failed a test—and what a test to fail. These tests would determine the extent of the injury as it related to my verbal memory, vision, spatial ability, intelligence, language (speech, reading, writing) and cognitive processing such as problem solving, planning, organizing, selective attention, and short-term memory.

It became apparent I had experienced a traumatic brain injury. When the doctor gave me my test results, he seemed visibly upset about how low I scored. The tests proved more serious than I, or even he, had imagined. He was amazed at how I had mastered getting around with this disability for ten months.

Despite the test results, the news gave me tremendous relief. Finally, a diagnosis! I was on my way toward recovery, although the journey ahead looked long and difficult. Nevertheless, my determination grew stronger. I would win this battle and make it even if the odds were stacked against me.

The doctor tried to explain that I wouldn't be the same and it would be extremely difficult to live in "mainstream society" again.

"That's okay," I said. "I know God has a plan for me."

I had no idea what the journey would be like. I just knew I would make it. How? My determination would prove him and the other doctors wrong.

RISING TO THE CHALLENGE

Living with a brain injury can be challenging as well as rewarding. I have learned who my true friends are and understand with compassion those who left when the road got too rocky.

I believe I experienced a better quality of life than I did before my accident. I had to relearn many tasks I was taught as a little girl, which forced me to see the world through a new pair of eyes, like I was "born again." I appreciated the abilities I had taken for granted, like tying my shoes, walking up stairs, making my bed. Each new learning opportunity came with the excitement of experiencing something for the first time and achieving what I didn't think possible. The only comparison I can make is when you see the excitement of a young child after tying their shoes for the first time. I've been given the opportunity to experience that thrill many times.

I left my life of being an overactive person to becoming someone who needed to sleep at least ten to twelve hours a night, including spending most of the weekends resting the entire day in a coma-like state and then get up and go to bed and sleep another ten to twelve hours. However, as my brain and body began to heal, my all-day naps became shorter.

After working an eight-hour day at the office, I came home to rest and relax. Keeping the house pretty quiet and the lights dim helped to take the daily pressure off my head and brain. I created a regular sleep schedule, which seemed to help quite a bit. Usually a good eight to ten hours of sleep each night enabled me to wake up without an alarm clock in the morning and provided me with the rest I needed to make it through each day at the office.

I'm sure you are asking, "How did she work with a brain injury?" I will explain in the chapters ahead.

LIFESTYLE CHANGE

Life meant having to adjust my lifestyle quite a bit. If I went out in the evenings on the weekend, I had to take a nap in the afternoon to ensure I could handle it. Before the accident, I never took a nap and wouldn't have even understood the need, but naps soon became a way of life for me.

Eating three healthy meals a day became another important adjustment to my new way of life. My body and brain knew exactly the hour for lunch and dinner and when I needed more fuel. One could have set their clock by me. If I didn't eat on time, my mind became very confused. I would get extremely tired and have difficulty breathing.

Before the accident, I could go all day without eating and never feel hungry. My body and brain were in such an adrenaline rush 24/7 that my brain never received the signals needed to tell me to slow down and eat.

After the accident, my lifestyle changed to becoming a more laid-back person. Friends and family reading this might be laughing, but I am really more laid-back now than before the accident. I no longer got adrenaline rushes. My empty stomach would now tell my brain it was hungry and needed to be filled. The hungry sensation became a new amazement on this journey since I rarely experienced it before the accident due to my busy schedule. My neurologist taught me about adrenaline filling up my stomach and why I was now starting to experience hunger pangs at the normal lunch and dinner hours. He helped me to connect all the dots.

I believe sometimes the accident was much harder on friends, coworkers, and family than on me since most of my early days and years in this condition were spent in a fog. While I don't remember much, those around me were watching, observing, and experiencing the reality of the devastation. A coworker friend drove me to work; other coworkers made sure I went to lunch and escorted me to meetings.

Unfortunately, being continuously in a fog or out of it caused me to be unaware of how I appeared to others. One coworker said that if he hadn't known better, he'd have thought I was strung out on cocaine. My face was expressionless, my skin pale, my eyes glassy, and most of the time I didn't even recognize coworkers' names or faces. Friends would share with me later that I wasn't even able to smile or laugh for many years. How do you forget to smile and laugh, especially when my smile is what people typically noticed? Coworkers told jokes, and I couldn't understand why everyone was laughing. I thought the joke must not be funny, or it went over my head.

During this time in my life, the comedy show *Seinfeld* was very popular. I remember watching it every week before the accident and laughing out loud. Watching it after the accident, I thought, this show isn't funny anymore. One of the guys who worked for me would come to work the next day after the show aired and reenact it. My team would be laughing in the office, and I thought, *What is it with these guys? The show is just not funny.* Only later would I realize that the reason I wasn't getting the humor was because I didn't understand what was being said.

WORKING CHALLENGES

At the office, I walked into cubicle walls because my spatial ability had been dramatically impaired. I'm sure I must have been a sight to see because prior to the accident, my coworkers saw me running around the office leading teams and in total control. After the accident was a whole different story. I needed assistance for almost everything I did. During the first several months, since I hadn't been properly diagnosed yet, nobody probably knew anything was wrong. That included myself, who only existed moment to moment.

Because I played a leadership role at work and was in charge of the project we were implementing, everyone needed to figure out how the work was going to get done while my brain had "left the building." I am truly blessed to have had bosses who cared about my well-being and worked hard to support me and protect my reputation by not sharing what had happened to me with everyone. Many within the organization were unaware of my injury or limitations.

I was also fortunate to have a strong team who could take over in my absence. I was proud and relieved when they rose to the challenge and carried on with only limited support from me. At the time, I don't believe they felt they could.

I'll never forget the day I sat in a conference room with my team and explained I had been diagnosed with a brain injury and didn't know if I would ever be the same again. I shared with them what I felt I could do and where I would need help from them. This was extremely difficult for a person who was always totally independent and never asked for help. Asking for and admitting that I needed help turned out to be the first of many tough moments to come. Even today I can still feel the emotion as I sat there facing my team and sharing about an unknown journey we were all about to embark upon, how I couldn't do this alone and needed their help to get me through the days ahead.

I know God puts people in our lives at certain times for certain reasons, and I am truly blessed to have had these coworkers at one of the most critical times. They are more than just coworkers; they are my friends—the ones who got me through each day both professionally and personally. It felt as if an army had been deployed to watch over me. Someone was never far away.

If we went to a meeting, someone would escort me to the conference room. I'm sure they were worried I might have trouble finding my way around the office and become easily lost or confused. When I had to carry something (we typically had big heavy binders of material), someone would carry my paraphernalia for me (carrying a heavy binder put extra pressure on my head and tired me out). They made sure I always had a seat. If standing, someone would bring me a chair. Sitting takes less energy than standing—amazing what you learn. Whenever we had a fire drill at the office, someone immediately came and escorted me out of the building. I often wondered if they had secret meetings to divvy up their roles—you take any fire drills, I'll take lunch duty, you make sure she leaves on time to go home, etc.

One of my coworker friends gave me a hug each day and always seemed to know when I needed someone around. A teammate was charged with running interference from a consultant who was really challenging to work with. This consultant had the type of personality that would totally exhaust a healthy person, and my teammate knew he would completely wipe me out. She would intercept him and handle all his questions and issues when we knew he was in the building.

When I look back at that time in my life, I am completely amazed and overwhelmed at what these folks did to personally help me in my recovery. I know I will never be able to thank them enough. If it hadn't been for them, I don't believe I would have recovered as well as I did. Someday, I hope to have the chance to show them how much I appreciated what they did. Some within the organization, I've lost touch with over the years, but I hope they will read this book and know the role they played in my life, what an awesome journey it has been, and how I've turned out perfectly. Today, my incredible team continues to help me through the challenges I face. They are always nearby or a phone call away to guide and support me.

MY FAVORITE VACATION—SKIING

My friends tried hard to encourage me in normal everyday activities and continue living life the way I did before the accident—even if that means continuing to go skiing every year, something I had done for many years. Skiing! Were we out of our minds?

Nevertheless, my one friend, Elaine, who saw me through this journey from the beginning, decided we would go to our favorite ski resort by ourselves. We planned the vacation with just ourselves instead of a group. A group would have been too much for me to handle. Plus, it was embarrassing to struggle physically and mentally in front of others. With the existing pain in my head, I couldn't even imagine being in the ski resort's condo with five other people talking and making any type of noise that would vibrate inside my head and cause more pain. Even someone moving around the room caused my brain to shoot into overdrive.

We went a couple of months after the accident. It was before I had been officially diagnosed with a brain injury. My friend surmised something wasn't right with me and suggested we go skiing like we did every year in March. She would make the plane, condo, and transportation reservations, as well as carry the suitcases and ski equipment (I didn't have the ability to lift or carry anything of weight as it put pressure and pain on my head.) Doing all that, she also had to keep her eyes on me, never knowing if I would become confused, wander off and get lost, or get tired and end up sitting in the middle of the airport floor. Can you even imagine taking me on a trip? It must have been equivalent to traveling with a little child.

Our first trip was to Breckenridge, Colorado, my favorite place. I always found ski vacations peaceful and relaxing, although I'm sure my friend would not have called this a relaxing vacation. Elaine had to carry two sets of luggage, two sets of skis and two sets of ski boots. She needed to help me on and off the plane as I could only walk with shuffled steps at a pace of 0.8 miles per hour (we actually timed me on a treadmill). I truly believe a 90-year-old grandmother could have passed me by with ease. Elaine became very protective of me, ensuring I didn't get bumped or hit on the head while passengers were putting their suitcases in the overhead.

Upon arrival, she needed to find some place for me to sit while retrieving our luggage, rent a car, pack the car with all our stuff, and then finally set off for the hour or so journey to the ski house we rented for the week. Since I was still having trouble walking, she did all this work even knowing there might be a chance I wouldn't be able to get on skis. Can you imagine me going down a ski mountain?

It still amazes me how Elaine walked next to me at such a slow pace. I had no idea until years later just how slow I really walked. Anytime we had to walk somewhere, the destination felt like miles away. It was challenging, exhausting, and overwhelming, and made getting around very difficult. The time it took to get from point A to point B felt like an eternity.

Our one-week vacation consisted of me lying on the couch, instead of skiing and staring out the window of our condo that over-looked the mountains I loved so much. I didn't have the ability to get off the couch, but had a beautiful view to look at each day that flooded me with emotion and joy at being able to see the crystal blue sky and the gorgeous white snow-covered mountains. Even though I didn't get to ski, which also filled me with some sad emotions, this trip did help me mentally. It brought me one small step closer to my victory in overcoming the challenges of living with a brain injury.

NEXT SKI VACATION

The next year, my friend and I decided to book another ski vacation, this time knowing I definitely had a brain injury. In my mind, I thought this time I would ski down the mountain, as my body was stronger since attending physical therapy three times a week. This sounded perfectly logical to me; however, I'm sure my friend was convinced otherwise. I believe she felt in her heart that taking me to the mountains would help me mentally and keep my spirit believing

I would recover. Unfortunately, reality showed it would be a long time, if at all, before I skied down a mountain.

This time, rather than lying around, I was able to walk outside the condo, put ski boots on my feet, and go to the mountain wearing my outfit. We had lunch at the bottom of the mountain and watched the skiers come down the hill. It was both thrilling and heartbreaking at the same time—thrilled at my latest accomplishment and knowing I was closer to my goal of skiing down the mountain, but heartbreaking to watch others doing what I believed I couldn't do anymore.

Tears and emotions hit both of us for different reasons, but mostly about the unknown as to what the future would hold. While my memory of this moment is about people skiing, both our memories are different.

My friend's recollection is watching me completely zoned out sitting outside with my back against a wall and sleeping. Since I lived moment to moment, I remember small moments that appeared huge and lifelike, such as wearing my ski boots, feeling the warmth of the sun beating on my face and body, and watching skiers fly down the mountain with ease. I'm so glad God has the ability to protect us from the bad memories. I know I don't have a recollection of all the struggling times. My friend, I'm sure, has sad memories etched in her mind of a vibrant young woman struggling in life.

Throughout the years and on these vacations while living with the brain injury, my friend continued to keep my spirits up by reminding me how far I had come, how I should keep believing that I would ski down that mountain one day real soon. I'm glad I didn't get depressed during my recovery, as I'm sure it would have set me back. I'm not saying I didn't have my boo-hoo moments, but overall I never really let my situation get the best of me.

EIGHT YEARS LATER

It took eight years, but I finally got skis on my feet and skied down the mountain! Of course, the first piece of equipment I put on was a helmet. But what an unbelievable feeling—the wind in my face and the mountain ahead of me and the excitement of being able to move faster than I could walk. It felt like flying! My cares, pain, and challenges were far behind me as I flew down the mountain on an easy slope, although not as fast as I usually did. It still felt like soaring to me. What an incredible, freeing experience.

I can never forget that first moment standing on top of the mountain looking down—I felt like I was on top of the world! Tears filled my eyes, and my body shook with disbelief at the view—something I had been dreaming about doing for several years. When I close my eyes, I can still see that view.

I had accomplished my first major goal since the accident and knew that nothing could stop my recovery. I would master this brain injury and truly be a survivor... I would live in "mainstream society."... I would beat the odds stacked against me... I would prove the doctors wrong. But my battle wasn't over yet. I had more tough experiences to tackle. Driving was one of them.

3

Facing Challenges Head-On

Driving is very challenging for a brain injury survivor, and I was very fortunate to have someone drive me to work each day. I hadn't driven for several months except to the doctor's office and back home again because there are so many distractions on the road and activities in the car to perform that challenge the brain. Driving for only 20 minutes exhausted me, and I would have to come home and rest for hours before being able to do anything else. It would take years before I could be out driving for an hour. This limited me dramatically. I am very blessed to have people in my life who do most of the driving for me, but it did limit where I could go by myself and kept me homebound for many years.

DRIVING...SOCIALIZING...TALKING...

During the many years after my accident, I traveled a major inter-state in New Jersey each day to work. This interstate was always bumper-to-bumper, and sitting in traffic surrounded by other cars gave me claustrophobic feelings that overwhelmed me. Being in tight or small spaces never bothered me before, but this feeling accelerated to a heightened level after the accident. Due to this, I had to find an alternate route to work so I could avoid traffic even if the route took a little longer.

Socializing was even more difficult for me than driving. Prior to my accident, I loved to be around people and attended parties and events. After the accident, I found this difficult. First, I couldn't understand what people were saying; their words sounded muffled and jumbled inside my head. Second, the environment around me was always swirling and spinning. My head ached, and I felt dizzy and disoriented. This period of time was extremely overwhelming, causing me to become isolated and spend most of my time in quiet and solitude. Friends soon began to slip away since I wasn't able to go out to social events such as the movies or parties.

Talking was also challenging, so I stopped speaking to people and calling them on the phone. The vibrations through the phone were painful, and I rarely understood what people were saying to me. Friends got upset with me because I didn't telephone them. My world became very lonely.

FRIENDS WHO NEVER LEFT

Two friends remained by my side and did not leave me during this journey. They took me places that wouldn't be too noisy and spent time with me. I'm sure they didn't really understand what was happening, but they adjusted their lives to accommodate what I was going through and didn't expect me to act or behave the same way I did before the accident. Other friends didn't understand that the thoughts I had prior to the accident were no longer in my mind. Time didn't really exist. I didn't know if I spoke to someone the other day or months ago. Nothing stayed in my short-term memory or moved into my long-term memory bank.

Many people with brain injuries lose their friendships. I'm not sure why, but I can imagine it is hard for others to watch what you are going through.

My two goddaughters were five months old and nine years old when I sustained the brain injury. I'm sure they really didn't understand what had happened, but that didn't matter to them. My friend Linda (their mother) brought them to my house, and they played with toys and games as I lay on the couch. As they got older, the youngest, Jessie, invented memory games for me to help strengthen my brain. She continued over the years to find ways to help my brain heal and grow. My oldest goddaughter, Lauren, closely observed and measured my progress. She commented to her mother that she saw me, Aunt Donna, walk up and down stairs versus taking the elevator and that she was confident I was getting better. This occurred many years after the accident. She also observed how long I stayed at their birthday parties or family events. The time I stayed was getting longer each time, and I began to participate in their conversations versus just sitting on the sidelines.

For Lauren, I'm sure this must have been a very difficult adjustment for her as I was very involved in the first nine years of her life. We did so many things together. We went to Sesame Place: Family Theme Park in Pennsylvania every year since her third birthday, the movies, out for ice cream, and even to amusement parks. Everything little kids did for fun, Aunt Donna and Lauren did together. Then almost in an instant my life changed, and I dropped out of her life. I'm sure she couldn't comprehend why I wasn't playing with her or spending time with her. You can't expect a nine-year-old to understand what many adults can't even comprehend.

One of my greatest joys occurred when Lauren wrote a paper about me for school. The assignment was to write about courage, and Lauren chose to write about my courage living with a brain injury. She kept what she wrote secret. We only found out afterward that I had been the topic, and my hope is one day to read what she wrote.

Another special moment happened when she had to complete her college application and write about someone or something that had influenced her life. Lauren again chose to write about the challenges I have faced. I am humbled and overwhelmed to think I could have made an impact on someone's life, especially someone who has been in my life for many years and is truly a special person to me.

Jessie, my youngest goddaughter, has such a precious soul. She was my caretaker and would always make sure I was okay and loved to play games with me. I remember playing the card game Concentration, where you had to remember the cards you turned over. I couldn't remember any of the cards I turned over. Well, with no short-term memory, it was easy for Jessie to win every game and beat me at a very young age. Many adults typically pretend not to remember when they play games with kids; I didn't have to pretend. I do believe these children's games were helpful in my recovery. Most of the time, it was extremely painful to play and totally exhausted me, but in the end I feel, it helped my brain regenerate and strengthen.

We continued over the years to play games, and she was always asking me questions and trying to come up with new games to help strengthen the areas of my brain that still needed to develop. When I would struggle to answer her questions, she would just say, "Aunt Donna, this is helping your brain." As she got older, she knew I had a brain injury and must have been intuitive enough to realize these games were helping me. I think she also overheard me say how I felt it was helping me.

For some reason, I couldn't seem to remember Jessie's age, and from year to year each Christmas, Jessie would receive a Christmas ornament from me with the number 3 on it. I guess my brain became stuck and she would always remain three years old in my mind. She continues to display the many Christmas ornaments, and we smile and reminisce how each year I bought her the same ornament.

The girls got a kick out of me when my tired brain made no sense when I spoke or said things backward. They would try to help me say the right words by finishing my sentences or making sugges-tions. At least I know they were listening and paying attention to me. Not many aunts can say they have the full attention of the children in their lives. I am truly blessed, but there were still more mountains ahead to climb.

Climbing the Mountain

I would love to someday actually climb a real mountain, but I don't yet have the physical strength needed to tackle that goal. I also wouldn't want to cause my friends and family to worry about me. I did, however, have an opportunity to take a chairlift up to the top of a mountain during my recovery, which helped me to feel like I actually did climb a mountain.

Simple tasks became monstrous events. How would I be able to live on my own and take care of myself? How would I pay the bills? How would I deal with little things when my brain wasn't working right? Take baby steps and ask for help—that would be the answer.

I would not have been able to climb the mountain to any height if it weren't for friends and family. There are so many people in my life who have helped me in ways they will never know. I'm sure there is much that people did for me that I don't remember, as my recollection of many of those years isn't very good.

I do know that the drive and determination of my type A personality, as well as my workaholism, helped me stay focused and determined to beat the odds. My can-do attitude didn't allow me to give up when at times I really wanted to. The overachiever in me wouldn't rest and be still while the world around me kept moving. I'm sure at times I pushed myself when I should have been resting to help my brain heal. I continually lived in a struggle to do more to help increase my endurance while, at the same time, trying to rest to help gain more energy.

The battle was constant. Do I take the stairs at work to help increase my motor skills and build endurance, or do I take the elevator to save energy for the rest of the day? These are thoughts and questions others don't have to think about or ask during the day but were on my mind constantly. At every moment, one decision I made could completely tire out my brain, or I could end up just fine. Sometimes that extra walk up the stairs could be the breaking point that created pain in my head that would last the rest of the day and night. The extra steps I took, or the conversation I had standing in the hallway, could knock me out for the rest of the day and night, causing a ripple effect. If I was too tired, the drive home could be challenging, which made me too tired to think about preparing dinner. The thought of eating would completely overwhelm me. Thus, the downward spiral began. Skipping dinner meant less energy and additional pain in my head. I'd go to sleep with a pounding migraine, and my sleep would be disruptive throughout the night. This made waking up for work the next morning even more challenging. I'm amazed at the smallest decisions that contributed to my downward spiral. Was it worth it?

Yes! Climbing the mountain is really worth it. Finding ways to continue to heal your brain and body is not only exciting but also extremely rewarding. Watching how much I improved over the years continued to help stimulate me toward complete recovery. Proving the doctors wrong? Priceless.

Anyone with determination, coupled with friends and family, can make this climb. It is important to listen to your doctors but even more important to listen to yourself. A doctor once told me to "manage through the pain." That was the best advice I could have gotten.

I constantly pushed myself to get better, but, at the same time, I would be careful not to overdo it. When exercising, walking, or working at my job, if I experienced pain inside my head, as long as it was tolerable I continued to push myself. This enabled me to tolerate the pain and to build endurance, which strengthened my brain and body. However, I would learn not to push too much so as not to cause total exhaustion and severe pain. It would be a never-ending balance.

If someone told me that I would be living with this brain injury for more than thirteen years, I probably wouldn't have believed them. But if I had known it to be true, I would have found it overwhelming and depressing. So I took it one day at a time and focused my attention on how much I grew and improved each day and year, making sure to take the time to celebrate the small milestones along the way.

I also set mini milestones as well as long-range plans. For example, if I want to climb a mountain, I would first set out to climb one-quarter of the way up by a certain date. Then, I begin to increase the distance until I reach the top. It is important to set realistic and attainable goals but also to set goals that will stretch you.

Some days it was easier to sit on the sofa and watch cartoons or a TV show that I had seen a hundred times. Lying on the sofa became comfortable and less painful, whereas going out into the real world was overwhelming and challenging. Little things like grocery shopping were exhausting and painful. It was scary to go out and interact with people knowing that my brain wasn't working properly. Sometimes just asking for help could be difficult when the words didn't come out right, sentences got tangled up in my mind, and the world was swirling in all different directions. People often looked at me funny and mocked what I said. During these times, inside my home was the only place I felt safe and secure.

As a brain injury survivor, I felt like I climbed a mountain almost every day. I am extremely blessed to have friends, family, and coworkers who also got excited for what seemed like baby-step accomplishments. These special people in my life became just as excited as I did when I walked up a flight of stairs, walked my first mile on the treadmill, attended my first concert without experiencing pain, or even rode the train for the first time alone to see my niece and nephew. My advice to all brain injury survivors is to accept the challenge and climb that mountain.

WHEN DOCTORS WOULDN'T LISTEN

While I have always had a healthy respect for doctors, many during my incredible journey were not helpful and caused me a lot of unnecessary emotional pain. What I've learned from this experience is that it is important to listen and pay attention to doctors, but it is just as important to know your own body and continue to push through the red tape and challenge if you are not getting answers to your situation. If I had listened and paid attention to many of the doctors, I would still be sitting on the sofa, doing nothing and missing out on this incredible life.

My first experience with a doctor who didn't listen was the neurologist I previously mentioned who I saw three weeks after my car accident. A coworker friend recommended her, knowing that my condition seemed to be getting worse and not better. After making an appointment, the first test the neurologist gave me was an EEG or electroencephalography. An EEG is like an EKG for the brain instead of the heart, and you are hooked up to many wires to test the brain waves. It is painless but messy for the hair. The test looks for tumors, strokes and measures the electrical activity of your brain.

While I was told the results weren't good, I have no idea what that meant or what they found. I only remember seeing this doctor weekly and providing her with a detailed account of my week—what I could and couldn't do, the constant shooting pain, and that something wasn't right with my head. I was forgetting things, struggling at work, completely exhausted, couldn't pay attention to conversations, kept walking into walls, and just wasn't myself. I would sit on the examining table while she sat at the opposite end of the room taking notes and saying nothing to me.

As I mentioned, each week I would leave with a new prescription to fill, and the only answer given me was that concussions take time to heal. I learned later that she continued to write down "headaches" in my chart when it wasn't a headache but a shooting, zapping type of pain in my head—totally different from a headache. The one positive outcome from months with this doctor was she put me in touch with her nurse, who taught me biofeedback. I explain this in the holistic approach section.

I left this doctor after she sued me because she hadn't received her payment in a timely fashion from the insurance company. Can you imagine a doctor treating a head injury patient and then suing them because they didn't get their payment on time? I was lucky to be getting to the appointments on time. Since my accident resulted from a car, the car insurance needed to pay all the medical bills, not my company's medical insurance carrier.

Now enters the second doctor who also didn't listen. As I mentioned, these medical bills were to go through the car insurance, and, of course, they wanted their own doctor to see me and provide a diagnosis. A friend came with me when I went to see this insurance-assigned doctor.

As the doctor asked me a series of questions, like my name, address, etc., I was able to quickly answer my name; however, responding with my home address at times was difficult to remember. Unfortunately, when this occurs, you begin to panic, knowing you should know the answer. This causes your brain to freeze, and your mind goes completely blank. Lucky for me, a friend quickly jumped to my aid and responded with the correct information. Strangely, when I struggled to answer this doctor's simple questions, he indicated in his report that I was perfectly okay. So now the car insurance would not pay the bills because I'm "okay," and my medical insurance company wouldn't pay either because it fell under the car insurance. Great! What a situation to be in—struggling with insurance companies and not having the ability to process what they were saying.

I believe at this time, since I didn't understand what was happening, I probably ignored letters or bills I was receiving—that is, until I got the lawsuit. Even with the brain injury, I quickly figured out this could be a serious situation. I found many times that I would ignore things that overwhelmed me, things I didn't understand or couldn't deal with just didn't get addressed. I'm sure in the back of my mind, I hoped they would go away.

I love how God places people in your life at the exact moment you need them. I happened to be working in the benefit department of my company when the accident happened, thus enabling me to be familiar with insurance companies and coworkers who would understand these bills. One of my coworker friends took all my bills and documents and worked with our company's insurance vendors to get all my bills paid. I know I will never know all the work and effort that went into getting these bills paid and getting the lawsuit to be dropped, but I will always appreciate that person and the help and support he gave me to make my life so much easier. Funny, this coworker friend is the father of the baby shower I was heading to when the accident happened. Small world, right!

Going forward, my medical journey would continue to be a challenge because every time I filled out a medical form describing my symptoms and indicating they were related to the car accident, I would continue to run into the same issue—car insurance versus company health care plan.

On to neurologist number 3. I'm several months into my journey, still in severe pain, totally exhausted, and all I know is I had a concussion in January, and it isn't getting any better. As the weeks and months progressed, it became more and more difficult to move my arms and legs and even difficult to lift my body out of bed in the morning. This next neurologist was the worst.

He treated me like I was some emotional female imagining all my symptoms. He was arrogant, sarcastic, and made me feel insignificant. When I asked him why he thought I was having trouble lifting my arms, he kind of snickered and said, "Why do you think you are having trouble"? Well, I thought, keeping it to myself, if I knew that, I really didn't need to be there. He immediately walked out of the room and came back and handed me a prescription for Prozac. Oh my gosh, can you imagine? This was his answer: "I'm giving you a drug because you are still depressed over the accident." Over an accident that happened almost six months ago? Totally unbelievable.

I left his office and sat in my car crying. Using all my energy just to get to a doctor's office and recount the last six months of my life— the pain, the challenges, the struggles—and leaving with another prescription to fill and no answers crushed my spirit. I called a friend. She became my go-to person and helped me to refocus whenever I received these kinds of devastating reports.

As I shared earlier, it was lucky for me I first needed to see a medical doctor for bloodwork before filling the Prozac prescription. I shared with my medical doctor my experience with this doctor, and he said, "I can tell just by talking to you that you aren't depressed and have a great handle on what has happened to you even though the full picture isn't known yet." He told me not to fill the prescription but decided to give me a blood test. It showed that my iron was low and I wasn't able to keep the iron vitamin in my system. This could explain the cause of my exhaustion. Finally, some answers to my symptoms. However, he still felt there was more than just being iron deficient but admitted that he had no experience with concussions. And at this point in time, we didn't know I had a brain injury.

Another doctor who didn't listen to me was my fourth neurologist. I met this doctor after being diagnosed with a brain injury. I wanted to understand why I still had severe pain in my head so many years after the accident. It had been more than ten years. I didn't want to live on medication since it only reduces or alleviates pain but doesn't cure it. I needed to know what was causing the pain. Again, no answer from this doctor.

My friend and I decided to go to New York City and seek answers at one of the top hospitals. Surely, we would find answers there, right? This time, my friend also decided to go with me into the examining room. She felt I might not be articulating all my symptoms correctly and wanted to tell the doctor what she's observed over the years and demand answers.

While in the doctor's office with all my notes and a detailed list of my symptoms, we were interrupted several times while he took phone calls. First, I found this behavior very rude, and, second, to do this to someone who has a head injury/concussion who has trouble focusing is totally insensitive. I struggled when he asked me basic questions, and during the examination when he physically tilted me back, my friend said I looked like I was completely out of it. My face had no color, and my eyes had no life to them—they were completely glazed over. Now how can a doctor say I'm okay!

Again, this doctor prescribed another type of medication. I told him I don't like taking medication, and he said that is the only thing they can do for the pain. But I said, "I want to know what is causing the pain." I couldn't believe what he told me. "You're doing too much and thinking too much. You need to rest your brain."

My response was this: "Well, how do I do that when I need to work and function?"

I decided to do what the doctor suggested and took the medication. It ended up making me so disoriented and even more out of it that I wasn't able to function. When I called to tell the doctor, he said, "Well, just cut the pill in half and only take half a pill."

This was getting me nowhere. These doctors just didn't listen or even try to understand what I was describing or attempt to find the root cause of the problem. Their solution was to just give me a prescription to fill. None of them could understand why I was so persistent about getting answers and getting back to being 100 percent. They just kept saying to me, "This is as good as it gets. You are at least functioning. You should be happy you aren't lying in a hospital." How could sleeping most of my days, not being able to socialize with friends and family, being confused and disoriented as well as living with severe pain be as "good as it gets"? How could sitting on a couch be "functioning"? This was not acceptable to me.

I finally made the decision to stop taking all the medication and try and manage the pain myself. I now have a huge bag of all the different medications doctors have prescribed for me during this journey.

My hero doctor came in the tenth month of my journey. He was absolutely shocked that the other doctors didn't listen to me. He would be the first doctor to truly listen to what I was saying and appeared to understand as I explained my symptoms and experiences. I believe it was at that moment that my determination to survive this experience turned into a passion to raise awareness and help others diagnosed with a brain injury. But in my determination, what would I now learn about the seriousness of this injury?

4

Finding Out This Was "Really Serious"

I think that unless you are hospitalized or in a coma, it is hard for others to realize how serious a brain injury can truly be. Many times people, as well as myself, would minimize the seriousness of my injury. From doctors to friends to family, I looked and appeared normal. Yes, there was something a little different about me but not as serious as what the tests would eventually reveal.

The one doctor who diagnosed me with the brain injury indicated he knew instantly by just talking with me and listening to my detailed description of experiences that there was something wrong. He chose at that moment not to put me through a series of exhausting tests and instead decided to give me a couple of simple tests, such as listing out 20 food items and asking me to repeat them. He also asked me to group shopping items together from memory, like clothes, food, etc. These should have been easy tasks to do; however, for someone with a brain injury, they are extremely challenging. I also had to copy a picture and then draw it from memory. The results of these simple tests showed that I fell below the 25 percentile, which meant the injury was significant. He based the tests on my age and

45

level of schooling, measuring them against others in the same category without a brain injury.

It would be years later that another doctor would run me through a series of more detailed neurological tests that would turn my world upside down and leave me totally devastated for the first and only time in my journey. I wasn't depressed where I needed medication or help—it was my positive, can-do attitude that suffered a direct hit. What happened?

REAL-LIFE EXPERIENCES VERSUS DOCTORS' TESTS

Eight years into my journey, my confidence had started to increase, and I was gaining confidence in my routine. I slept a lot, especially during the weekends, to recover from working a full week. I didn't really go out much except to do a little food shopping, but I was surviving. Around this time, the doctors wanted to see how significant the damage was to my brain. I took a series of tests lasting about eight hours.

These tests were painful for my brain as I really had to focus and concentrate for a long period of time. Being a good student in school, I always knew when I passed or failed a test, and it was easy to know if you studied or if you were just guessing at answers. The doctor's types of tests one couldn't study for, yet throughout the entire test, you knew instantly if you were passing or failing.

When the doctor put a picture of a current-day leader in front of me and I couldn't come up with the person's name, when I was asked to fill in a word to complete a sentence in front of me and I couldn't think of the word or even any word that would fit the sentence, and when I had to calculate a grammar school math problem and had to leave it blank, I knew instantly I was in trouble.

Prior to the accident, I excelled in math; it was one of my favorite subjects. I took calculus in college and ended up tutoring many of my classmates. Now fast-forward to sitting with a doctor asking

46

you to count backward from 100, and you get stuck at 99, and the doctor even helps you get started. Count backward? How could this be so difficult? Yet my brain would get stuck on the number 100 and not be able to move backward. The doctor tried to encourage me, saying, "Yes, you can do this." But the harder I tried, the more my brain got stuck and wouldn't move. Even as I write this, I can still feel the emotion of not being able to think and come up with the answer. I could feel the pressure of trying and my brain starting to feel more pain and pressure, after which my emotions kicked in. All you want to do is run away and cry. These tests were emotionally draining and devastating.

Some other tests included knowing the difference between fruit and vegetables. I didn't do well on this either, funny though I'm not sure if I even knew that information before the accident. Remembering people's faces was also challenging. I knew ahead of time I wouldn't have scored well in this area, as I had trouble both recognizing coworkers in the office and people in my personal world.

One time I ran into my dentist in a parking lot, and as he was talking to me, I stared at him like he was a stranger. I knew he spoke to me like I should know him. This set me into a panic, knowing I should know the guy and I didn't. It is so scary to talk to someone who knows your entire life and family, and you stand there wracking your brain, trying to figure out who the person is and why he is asking personal questions about your family. It wouldn't be until my yearly dentist appointment that I found out it was my dentist. He said he thought something was odd by the look on my face and was shocked to learn I had sustained a traumatic brain injury.

During my tests, the doctor would show me a series of faces and then another set of faces, and I had to remember if I recognized these faces from the first group he showed me. He would repeat the same exercise with a second group and then give me a combination of the first two groups. Each face was a blur to me—I wouldn't remember if I had seen these faces in either of the groups, or ever. It felt like my mind went to sleep while looking at these pictures—a total blank. It is so hard to articulate the emotions and feelings you experience when you are totally convinced you should know the answer and everything is a total blank.

These tests went on for about eight hours. Half way through these tests, I became very tired, which made taking the tests even harder to complete. My focus and concentration were impacted, which was one part of the design of the tests. By the end of the experience, I was completely exhausted, but the emotional side took an even bigger toll on me.

I was devastated to realize how serious the damage was to my brain when I couldn't pass any of the tests the doctor gave me. I can still recall staring at a blank piece of paper where mathematical answers should be and the face of the tester trying to encourage me in finding the answer to his questions. I didn't pass a single test he gave me. Each one seemed harder and harder. After each test, I would become more and more emotional. I knew I wasn't passing; no one had to grade this test—I knew instantly I did not pass. You can't leave questions blank and expect to pass. It was even harder and more embarrassing when the doctor was actually in the room giving the test and asking the questions. Now the embarrassment was even stronger as I sat face-to-face with the doctor, and inside my head I was feeling like a complete idiot. I had a lot of pride at that time. In the past, I always loved knowing answers to questions and typically acing tests. So you can imagine how upsetting and humiliating this experience was for me to be right in front of a doctor and not be able to answer simple questions.

Many of the other tests were timed, but you did it alone in the room. I think it is less embarrassing failing the test in the room alone than to feel unintelligent right in front of someone. What an awful experience to go through, and the worst would come when I received the final results. My mind raced with the realization that I use to be intelligent, an A student, and now I wasn't. What happened? I pass tests, I don't fail them! I'm a smart person; people come to me for answers. I can win the categories on the *Jeopardy* game show. What is happening that I can't remember Mount Rushmore when I see the picture? Or after being given a grocery list of 20 items, I can only remember the first two items on the list? Getting these results left me bewildered, embarrassed, and devastated all at the same time.

As I opened the envelope containing the results and read the ten-page document spelling out the shocking results, I remember being in total disbelief. The scores were not good. I thought I was doing well, getting better, functioning. I was getting up in the morning, going to work, and coming home. How could I have scored so badly? My results showed that I fell around the 5th–9th percentile of the different categories. I knew I struggled during the test, but 5 and 9 seemed to be good numbers. I thought they reflected I did well.

I asked a friend, "These are good scores, right?" *Yes* was the answer I hoped for.

I had a hard time grasping that the low scores could possibly be for my age and schooling, especially since I was still working and, I thought, functioning pretty well. Seeing these scores in black and white became a final straw for me emotionally. My mind was conflicted. They showed solid proof that my brain wasn't perfect. I wasn't the A student I used to be. I wasn't the smart person that so many knew me to be. I was someone with a disability. These pieces of paper were telling me something I never let myself believe from the beginning—that my brain was damaged and that I had a disability. The doctor even started his result's summary as, "She is a master at disguising her disability." Yes, I had not only been fooling people into believing I was fine, as well as myself. But now this piece of paper told me otherwise. I gradually became convinced that there was significant damage to my brain.

I'm sure it was hard for others to imagine or understand why at times I seemed to be able to function okay and appear normal and then within seconds not be able to figure out how much money to give a cashier to pay for my lunch. To compensate, I learned to keep twenty-dollar bills in my wallet so I didn't have to struggle to figure out how much something cost. By handing them a large bill, they would simply give me change. At the end of a week at work, I had an accumulation of a lot of singles in my wallet.

Many times I would have moments of clarity and sound just like the old me while at the same time be struggling to think of the right word or ask a silly question. I did exert a lot of energy trying to hide my disability. I became creative in figuring out ways to get around the tasks I couldn't accomplish. In retrospect, I believe this had a dual effect of helping as well as hurting my brain. By being creative, it stimulated my brain to keep striving to get better; however, at the same time, it tired out my brain and caused me tremendous pain.

It would take me almost three weeks to get over and process the ten-page report showing the results of the damage to my brain. Lucky for me, I quickly snapped out of the negative emotional state it threw me into when I met a group of other brain injury survivors. They enabled me to fight back and regain my confidence and can-do attitude by sharing my story with them.

WHAT HAPPENS WHEN YOUR PERSONALITY CHANGES

For me, one of the major negatives of the brain injury was the emotional and behavioral challenges that surfaced. Prior to the accident, I would have described myself as a person always in control of her emotions. They were kept in check, good or bad, knowing I could handle different situations that arose in my life. I would play out what-if scenarios in my head in order to be prepared for whatever life threw at me. After the accident, I came to realize that I no longer had the ability to control my emotions and had to learn how to adjust and handle these new experiences.

For example, riding in an elevator never bothered me in the past. After the accident, I would need to take elevators all the time, as I couldn't walk up stairs due to the pain in my head and physical limitations of climbing stairs. However, getting into an elevator wasn't easy. I experienced some form of claustrophobia where the walls felt like they were closing in on me, and I would feel the panic rise up inside of me as the doors closed, expecting them never to open. My mind played tricks on me, making me believe I would be trapped inside forever. I could hardly wait to get off as quickly as possible. When I realized this was occurring because my brain wasn't properly functioning, I had to try to keep myself calm and continue to tell myself that the doors would indeed open at my stop.

These were emotions I had never experienced before, and because my brain wasn't operating in a normal fashion, spaces of time weren't the same anymore. A simple ride up one level in the elevator seemed like an eternity, leaving me emotionally and physically drained. As you can imagine, these new emotions put extra stress and pressure on an already injured brain.

Even sitting in a plane or a car gave me an overwhelming feeling of being trapped and wanting to be in an open space or back in my house. I would have to learn how to force myself to do things outside of my new comfort zone; otherwise, I would have never been able to leave my house. I remember a 30-minute car ride felt as if I were driving cross-country. Friends would now have to come to my house, as I couldn't handle simple drives to their houses. Before the accident, these trips were quick and easy but now felt like a never-ending road trip. Trips to the grocery store, picking up takeout at a restaurant, or even a quick visit to a friend felt like an endless trip, so completely overwhelming that many times I would choose to stay home instead of going out.

My home became the only place where I felt comfortable and safe. I would be restless and uneasy at someone else's house, even if visiting for a short period of time. Why? I never knew when my brain would fail me or I would experience something I wasn't prepared to handle. Of course, at the time you don't realize this is what is happening; you just want to be lying down on your favorite sofa with a pillow and a blanket, watching the same TV show for the 100th time. Now I've come to understand that watching something familiar was easy and didn't force my brain to focus. It enabled my brain to relax and just enjoy. Watching something new overwhelmed my brain, and I couldn't follow the story line because it forced my brain to work harder by having to pay attention and focus in order to understand. This additional pressure on my brain caused fatigue and pain. This caused emotions to rise up inside of me with the feeling of being incompetent or stupid.

During this journey, for survival, I took on a self-centered nature. At first, I would continue to do what everyone else expected of me—that would ultimately wipe me out. One of my doctors encouraged me to tell others what I was experiencing and helped me to focus on what was best for me in every situation. Of course, this isn't one of my normal personality traits—focusing on my needs ahead of others. Here would be the dialogue I would now have with myself—focusing on my needs. Would I be able to handle a crowd of people? Could I make that long trip in a car? Would I be too tired to stay out at a party, etc.? Everything had a rippling effect on my body and brain.

To solve the problem, every event and activity had to first start with a list of questions and thoughts about how much any event could impact me at that moment as well as over the next couple of days. I now had to focus on what was best for me. However, I would find out that others didn't understand what I was going through and, I'm sure, didn't like the times I would say no or simply not attend a function. In the past, I never said no to anyone even if it was something I didn't want to do. Now my world became very small, with only me in it. It was something I had to do in order to survive the journey at that time.

Hopefully you can imagine how someone who is living with pain 24/7, who never feels their best and struggles with simple tasks, can at times become irritable. I would now start to experience this new behavior—feeling myself getting easily frustrated with people, which rarely happened to me in the past. I'm sure at times it was justified, but that didn't make me feel any better when I couldn't articulate my needs or try to explain why I couldn't do something. It feels similar to a young child who can't talk yet, and they throw a temper tantrum—they are trying to express something but just can't make it happen and get frustrated. That is how I would feel at times. I couldn't get my words or thoughts out or express what I needed, and it would boil up inside of me. You can see how this could get exasperating for someone who used to be great at articulating thoughts and ideas.

I found it interesting how during those times when I was over-tired, I would make negative comments. I can recall this happening at work from time to time. One of the guys I worked with thought this was funny since it was so contrary to my personality. I was viewed as the eternal optimist—the perky, happy person that sees the positive in everyone and every situation. I continued to try and see the good in everyone, even the not-so-nice ones; however, after a long day and sometimes after someone did something strange or aggravating, I could be caught saying something not so positive. Of course, this guy would happen to be with me and would smile, as he knew immediately I must be tired and that my filtering system hadn't stopped me in time to keep me from blurting out something negative. My team members said they enjoyed my negative outbursts, even if out of character, because it made me human. Good news for me that my coworkers knew my heart was kind and knew I didn't really mean what came out of my mouth. They also knew that if I became aware of what I had said about or to someone, I would feel bad. I'm so glad I didn't use profanity or engage in inappropriate behavior. This does happen to many brain injury survivors. I feel so blessed that I could continue to be around people and not experience emotional outbursts or behaviors that raised attention to my disability.

Practically every morning, I would wake up and feel completely exhausted, even after a good eight hours of sleep. Getting ready for work in the morning took a couple of hours, as I would need to factor in many rest periods. Each activity would tire me, leaving me breathless, thus causing me to take a break in between and simply sit on the bed and rest before tackling the next activity.

Just getting out of bed, I would have to sit for a few minutes with the TV on to help stimulate my brain. The next step would be taking a shower and then a 20-minute rest before attempting to get dressed, put on makeup, and blow-dry my hair. In the past, while on ski trips, my friends were always amazed at how quickly I could be dressed and ready in my full ski outfit in less than 30 minutes. Now, getting ready for work took a couple of hours.

Before leaving for work, I would ensure I ate breakfast, and then the journey would begin of needing to spend time in the bathroom for a while, as my body seemed to react to food in the morning. This was my other challenge, especially when tired—I had trouble digesting my food. This caused some issues. Let's just say I became very knowledgeable about different bathroom locations along my route to work. I would wait until feeling okay before proceeding in the car to the office. Then there were the times when I would need to urgently stop along the way to find a restroom. I remember one time so clearly when I had to stop at a preschool. As I walked in, I must have looked really bad, as the teacher let me use the kids' restroom and kept all the kids away until I resurfaced. I have no idea what this was all about, but to me it became a way of life each morning for many years. Often, I would have sweat pouring down my face and the feeling of clothes on my body was agony.

Sometimes, when I got too tired or had to be somewhere quickly, such as trying to catch a plane, my symptoms would occur. Trying to rush my body on a timetable caused it to react. However, if I went at the pace my body dictated, I was okay. Needless to say, you can imagine how challenging this can be when you need to travel somewhere and try to live in mainstream society.

Eating out or at someone's house was challenging, as I had to be careful what I ate. Salads were hard to digest, and being tired or not eating on time, plus too much noise stimulation, multiple conversations at the same time, or a lot of people in the room, caused my brain and body to have a strong negative reaction. It could be especially embarrassing if I had to run to the bathroom or my body and brain didn't react in a normal fashion. I never wanted anyone to see me in these types of conditions and continually worried about what people would think and say if they saw me act out of character.

Even in my own home it was uncomfortable if I had people in my house and started to not feel well. I always wanted to appear perfectly normal. Ugh, even remembering these experiences brings up memories of not-so-fun times. I put a lot of pressure on myself by trying not to show my disability or the challenges I faced on a daily basis.

I believe one of the biggest challenges for my friends and family was that I never called people on the phone. The reason? Talking on the phone hurt my head. Between the vibration of the phone against my ear and having to pay attention and listen, it was also exhausting for me to talk.

Now I know my friends and family who are reading this are saying, "Yeah, right." Let me explain. It might appear effortless to talk, but while living with the brain injury, it takes a lot of energy to talk and hold a conversation. Once I finished, I would be exhausted, and the pain in my head would increase, leaving me tired, drained, and in pain. My doctor shared with me that the speed at which I spoke and the intensity zapped more energy. He did try to get me to slow down and speak softer, but that wasn't an easy task for me, especially when I would get excited about a topic or energized by just being with someone. I am an off-the-charts extrovert and am energized by talking and being with people, which before the accident and even at the moment appeared okay. However, it would completely wipe me out afterward and would take me a long time to recover.

My challenges regarding space and time impacted my friends and family because they couldn't understand. Seconds, minutes, hours, days, months, weeks, years all felt the same to me because I lived moment to moment. If you said to me, "I just saw you last week," it wouldn't register in my brain. If someone said to me, "You haven't called me in a month," I am unable to comprehend that span of time. So when I didn't call friends and family that I typically spoke with before the accident, they felt like I was blowing them off or didn't care when in reality I wasn't aware of the length of time in between phone calls or get-togethers.

These challenges would turn into new journeys I would experience with friends as well as alone. Would these new journeys be life changing and help further my ultimate goal of surviving this brain injury?

5

Journey Experiences

Years of living with my brain injury produced different kinds of experiences. At times, they left me humbled, frustrated, scared, overwhelmed, and struggling to comprehend what was happening. I'm sharing a few of these experiences not only to help you understand my journey but also to raise awareness for those survivors who might not be able to articulate what they are living through.

GETTING TO KNOW THE "NEW" ME

I found during this journey that I became a "new" person. The quicker I accepted the new me, the easier the journey became. Yet at the same time, I missed the "old" me. I knew and understood her well. I knew what she could and couldn't do, her strengths and weaknesses, her likes and dislikes. On the other hand, this "new" person was a complete mystery. I had to spend time getting to know the "new" me. This was not an overnight accomplishment. It took years of mourning the "old" me and learning to embrace the "new" me. This isn't easy for any brain injury survivor. This became even more

57

evident at a support group I spoke at for brain injury survivors. The facilitators for the group were occupational therapists I met along my journey. They loved my attitude and felt it would benefit other survivors they were supporting. They asked me to share my story in the hope of helping others see how far I had come in my journey and how I functioned day to day.

A woman at the group shared how she held a very high-level executive position and had been fired after they learned she had a brain injury. She spent almost an hour talking about the position she held and complained about what she used to be able to do. I could tell instantly that she did not want to let go of the past and grieve her "old" self. She had not embraced her new life.

I shared with her and the group how much I missed my "old" self but learned to embrace my new life and also find new traits to like about myself. I cherished my new accomplishments and shared how I kept a record of them, like climbing a flight of stairs instead of having to take the elevator, being able to run errands for more than ten minutes, and achieving the ability to make my bed in the morning. I'm not sure why making a bed proved so physically exhausting for me except to say that leaving my bed unmade seemed, at the time, not to be the end of the world. I didn't tackle that chore until many years after the accident.

After sharing my journey with the group, I could see the impact of my life experiences register in the faces of those women, especially the former executive in particular. I could see it in her eyes, like a lightbulb had suddenly gone off inside her. She really understood what I had shared and that she realized she needed to embrace her new journey and not focus on her former life.

What an awesome experience to be able to impact the life of someone who had been struggling with a similar journey. The facilitators were thrilled with the outcome because that was their motivation for inviting me to the group—to bring hope to others who were struggling with similar issues.

I am so blessed that God equipped me with a positive, can-do attitude. Throughout my life, I have always tried to see the positive in any given situation. Fortunately, I didn't lose this attitude while living with my brain injury. While I did struggle emotionally at times, my pity parties never lasted more than an hour or two—except when the doctors continually had me take a series of cognitive tests for many years during my journey. These are the tests I mentioned earlier that left me emotionally drained and struggling for several weeks—that is, until this moment when I found out my journey could help impact others. It gave me a strong sense of purpose for my life.

HANDICAP STICKER

In the beginning of my brain injury journey, I did not realize I had so many challenges. Why? Because I lived moment to moment, surviving through each of my experiences. Parking, for example, never seemed to be an issue as there were available parking spots near my house and the building where I worked. This made it easy for me to remember where I had parked my car. The close proximity enabled me not to have to walk any long distance, which would have tired me out before my day began or ended.

Many years after the injury, my work office moved to the original building where I had started my career. While I was so excited to be going back to that building, I had no idea it would present me with a new challenge. The large campus would leave me parking my car a long distance from the building. It also included a hill I would have to tackle at the end of my workday. During this time, I still had trouble walking up inclines.

I decided to give it a try because I wanted to be like everyone else and didn't want any special treatment. This would be the first time I had to walk a distance to work or anywhere.

The walk to the building in the morning wasn't too bad—it did take me a while as my steps were short and slow—but leaving in the evening was overwhelming. I struggled in pain trying to get up the huge hill. While to others it would appear as only a little incline, to me it felt like climbing Mount Everest. Once up the incline, there were hundreds of cars in this parking lot that completely short-circuited my brain. This caused pain, confusion, and an overwhelming panic within me. I had no idea how to find my car. My eyes would dart from side to side while the inside of my brain was spinning, trying to process what my eyes were trying to see. Even when I had written down a description of the location and where I had parked my car, the layout of the parking lot was too difficult for my brain to process. It is very difficult to articulate this and what my brain and body were experiencing. Just know that because my eyes and brain were not able to locate my car, panic and disorientation quickly took over.

My friends encouraged me to talk with the real estate supervisor and the medical department to see what they could suggest. While I didn't want any special treatment, the pain and total exhaustion every day was not good for me, so I reluctantly went and asked for help.

I can't say they were helpful. This was my first experience with people in my working environment who discounted my challenges and struggles and treated me with little respect. In all my previous work locations, the leadership and people went out of their way to make me feel comfortable asking for help.

I explained my situation and challenges to them and asked for suggestions where to park my car. Their solution? Ask my doctor to authorize a handicap sticker. This suggestion did not sit well with me at all, as I never considered myself handicapped. After all, I could walk. I just needed a consistent place to park my car that didn't involve an incline or hill. I'm sure they were trying to help and may have been sensitive to my situation; however, I had never needed a handicap sticker, and this really upset me. It hit me in the face and highlighted that I wasn't totally 100 percent myself. Prior to this, whenever possible I had tried to hide and keep my disability secret, not that I was embarrassed by being a brain injury survivor but more from the perspective that I wanted to believe I could handle all these types of challenges and didn't need special treatment. It was more of a pride issue. I didn't want to park in a handicap spot!

The best place to park my car would naturally be right in front of my building where the handicap signs were located. I knew my doctor would sign the appropriate paperwork, but besides my pride,

I also felt tremendous guilt in taking a spot away from someone who, in my mind, needed the space more than I did. Another reason? I knew I looked perfectly normal, and I thought people would judge me without really knowing why I needed to park in this space.

I spoke with my doctor, and he immediately completed the necessary paperwork enabling me to receive a permanent handicap sticker. Each morning, I would hang it on my rearview mirror and park in the exact same spot. For a while it was hard to do, but it proved a little bit easier when the weather was cold or rainy. The new parking situation made a huge difference in my energy level, especially at the end of a long day at the office. Plus, my coworkers continually emphasized how great it was for me to be able to park so close, thus making me feel special rather than handicapped.

I only used this sticker during my days at the office. I was determined not to get lazy and use it other times. There were many times while shopping that I could have taken advantage of the sticker to get a great spot but decided that if I was out running errands, then I was strong enough to park and walk to my destination even if it did take me a while.

I didn't really go far during these days and could always find my car because I purposely tried to park in the same general spot every time. Only once did I use the handicap sticker outside of the office. Friends drove me to a Billy Graham event where there were thousands of people. We would have had to walk miles from the general parking area—which I could not have done physically—but were able to park in the handicap lot and be escorted to our seats. Taking advantage of the sticker enabled me to save up more energy to spend with my friends, hear Billy Graham speak, and understand what he was saying. Without it, I would have completely been overwhelmed and in pain, thus spoiling the event for me and my friends.

That experience taught me that at times, it's okay to ask for help. My persistence in always wanting to appear like there was nothing wrong with me encouraged my friends and me, but it also caused a lot more pain, and I would tire easily because of my charade. I had to accept the fact that I had limitations and that there was nothing wrong with having this handicap sticker and using it when I needed it the most. I have, however, learned not to focus on the word *handicap*. While I don't believe there is anything wrong with being handicapped, for me personally, I did not want to become lazy and use it as a fallback position. I also feared being labeled. To me, words are important, and it is easy to become branded as lazy, incompetent, or stupid. Words like these can hurt someone who is trying to get back on their feet and live in mainstream society. Hanging this sticker on my rearview mirror each day caused me to feel defeated in my journey, and I had to work each day not to feel defeated. Removing the handicap sticker many years later from my car would be an incredible moment in my journey toward healing.

TRIP TO NIAGARA FALLS

A friend and I traveled to Niagara Falls for several days to see the beautiful waterfalls. We had a great window view of the falls from our hotel room, which would work out perfectly for me just in case I wasn't feeling well or strong enough to physically go to the falls.

We rested after our long drive and then set out to walk around the town. At this point in my journey, my walking speed had increased a little faster than the 0.8 mile per hour I was accustomed to; however, I still wasn't at a normal walking pace. We took a nice slow, leisurely walk until we came to a hill or incline. I'm not sure why, but physically I could not make it up inclines or hills. If you've ever been to Niagara Falls, you know there are a lot of hills and inclines. There was also an incline, a ramp from the street to our hotel room that presented a huge problem for me.

My friend and I stared at the ramp, and then we looked at each other, thinking, "How are we going to do this?" My friend jokingly said, "Try walking backward up the ramp." We both had previously worked with a gentleman that walked backward at the office. We understood that he had some medical issue with his brain that caused him to walk backward. So I tried it. Sure enough, I got up the ramp without any pain in my head or trouble with my legs or body. We were both laughing and surprised at the same time. This opened up a lot of new opportunities.

Even though I could now walk up inclines and ramps backward, I still struggled with endurance because I had a tendency to push myself to the point of total exhaustion. As we were walking around the area near the falls, my body and brain decided they had had enough and just decided to stop working. I sat down on the curb and couldn't move anymore. It felt like someone had unplugged me, my battery had run out of juice, and nothing worked inside of me. I wasn't even able to converse with my friend. Luckily, we were on a sidewalk the first time this happened.

To her, I had completely zoned out and wasn't aware of anything happening around me. I appeared to be asleep with my eyes open, no expression on my face, no appearance that anyone was home—physically there but not mentally. When my friend spoke to me, there was no acknowledgment, so I'm sure I didn't even hear her talking to me. She just patiently sat there with me waiting until my brain and body woke back up. I'm not sure how long this took, but I am truly blessed to have such a patient friend to sit by my side and wait. She never appeared to panic, but I'm sure that inside she was thinking, "What am I going to do if she doesn't wake back up? How will I get her back to the hotel?" Lucky for her, I had zoned out before and always woke back up. So she just sat there watching the falls and praying I would wake up shortly. I had no recollection or memory of that moment until later when my friend told me about it.

Our next experience at Niagara Falls occurred at a malt shop. I love milkshakes and 1950s' soda shops. As we walked around the town, we found a '50s' soda shop. We sat at one of the tables, looked at the menu, and decided to get lunch and a milkshake. My friend, at this point of my journey, thought I should try to do some things on my own. Since the accident, my friends did everything for me. She told me to go up to the counter and ask for a vanilla milkshake. Sounds pretty simple, right? Well, it wasn't.

At the counter, the waitress asked me a question. I stood there completely clueless and helpless. I had no idea what this woman had asked. When that happens, it is like someone is speaking in a garbled language. It doesn't even sound like a foreign language—only a muffled sound. The best example of this is the *whomp, whomp, whomp* sound that is used when the teachers or parents in the *Peanuts* cartoon would talk to the children. You never heard the adults speak; you only heard *whomp, whomp whomp*. That is exactly what I often heard when someone would ask me a question, or even when people were talking in a conversation. My friend, watching from a short distance, immediately came to my rescue.

At times like this, your emotions go through a lot. I used to be an intelligent person. How could I stand there and not be able to understand a simple question? How could I be an adult and so help-less? Why can't I comprehend what this person is asking me? Why do I feel like I'm stuck and trapped inside my head? These moments leave you emotionally embarrassed and devastated.

The simple question the woman behind the counter had asked me was whether I wanted soda pop or milk with my milkshake. In Canada, you have that option instead of milk. Thankfully my friend answered the question, and I received my vanilla milkshake and enjoyed it. Another crisis averted because someone knowledgeable was at my side to handle what would appear to be a simple question or situation but to me an impossible task. Unfortunately, these expe-riences leave an indelible imprint that cause brain injury survivors to not want to step out in public again and to shy away from tackling anything on their own. It is a major problem because one may appear perfectly fine—not a bump or scratch on you and no outward signs that show the world there is something wrong inside your brain.

Trying to function in mainstream society is challenging when someone asks you a question, and you don't understand and aren't able to respond, or when you're trying to ask a question, and your words get twisted, and your sentences don't amount to anything that makes sense to others. Fortunately, most of the time, someone was alongside of me and could interpret my comments or ques-tions. These challenging experiences limited me from attending social engagements. I didn't want to be around others where I might embarrass myself and my disability would be visible. As mentioned earlier, I constantly tried to hide my disability—not because I was ashamed of my new life but because people didn't understand and had a tendency to judge me harshly and unfairly.

SLEEPING ON A BENCH

While vacationing in St. Augustine, Florida, a friend and I had another fun moment while sitting on a bench. St. Augustine has a beautiful scenic shopping area near a fort where you can find great gifts and souvenirs. On this particular day, I felt a little tired and didn't have the energy or strength to walk around but was disappointed for my friend who loves to shop.

We decided to leave me sitting on a bench where she could keep an eye on me while she went gift shopping. I have no idea how long I sat there, but I must have zoned out again. When she came to check on me, she found me sitting upright, perfectly straight with sunglasses on, so no one would have been the wiser that something might be wrong with me.

She spoke to me, and I did not respond. She figured me to be asleep while sitting and having no clue life was going on around me. Even an elderly man came and sat down next to me, and the entire time, I was unaware of his presence. He probably tried to talk to me and I didn't respond. I must have looked like a statue. My friend said she came back to check on me several times, and each time I stayed in this statue-like state. She couldn't get any reaction from me or even wake me up. When my brain and body were ready, I finally woke up and returned to the world. This was not an uncommon occurrence.

Plopping down at random happened many times. I gradually became sensitive to when my body and brain needed to rest, and I would just plop down anywhere and not move until my brain and body decided to work again. You would be surprised where I found places to sit and rest. It never mattered to me if it were a bench, the grass, concrete sidewalk, or a mall floor—they all worked for me. I'm sure my friends have many funny stories about something I've said or done over the years. I'm so glad we all had a good sense of humor during those times; otherwise, it could have been a much longer and painful journey. Looking back on my journey, my memory is only that it has been incredible.

WHAT TO DO WHEN THE LIGHTS GO OUT

One summer day, I came home and knew that something didn't seem right in the house. I flipped on a light switch, and nothing happened. All I can remember is calling my friend for help. This became a constant in my life when something happened that I didn't understand. She had to magically figure out the situation from a distance. After determining that the power was out, she then helped me figure out my next steps.

First, she guided me in finding candles and a flashlight. I'm sure she really didn't want me lighting candles as I could have easily forgotten to blow them out. How fortunate that she knew enough about my house to direct me in finding what I would need if the lights didn't come back on in time. It was a nice warm summer day, so the air conditioner was also off. She instructed me to open the windows, sit outside, and prepared me for the possibility of being in the dark when nighttime came. This proved to be a major catastrophe for me.

This would be my first time experiencing being in the dark since the brain injury—and new experiences are always a little challenging and scary. As I sat outside on my deck, watching and listening to my neighbors in the area, everyone seemed to be moving around like nothing had happened. To me, having the power out felt like a huge deal. Anything out of the ordinary took on a magnitude that wasn't always realistic. While sitting outside, I wanted to yell out to my neighbors, "Don't you know the power is out? Why are you walking around like nothing is wrong?" Inside I felt anxious and jumpy, but everyone else seemed to be taking this in stride. I couldn't understand why there wasn't panic in the parking lots outside my condo. Why weren't people running around? That was my frame of reference and the feelings that were stirring inside me.

It is hard to explain how inside your mind and body, it feels like a major catastrophe has hit while reality shows it to be something different. I later learned that the anxiety and nervous feelings are common for brain injury survivors, as well as learning how to keep those emotions and feelings calm at best. Having an understanding helped me to deal with these types of experiences whether it impacted me physically, mentally, or emotionally. Once I understood, I was able to figure out the coping skills I needed to handle any given situation. It almost became a fun challenge—I said *almost*. I tried not to let my experiences or situations bring me down and tried to tackle them head-on. I do have to say, though, not everything was easy and perfect. I had my moments when I thought something was too hard and I couldn't do it any longer and wanted to give up and quit—sleeping on the sofa would be so much easier. However, most of the time, I could pick myself up and conquer the mountain facing me.

Eventually the lights came back on—a transformer had blown in the neighborhood. From that moment on, I kept a battery-operated light next to the sofa and one next to my bed and quickly learned that whenever the lights went off to just tap this light and I would no longer be in the dark. Thank goodness I am a teachable person. It became a continuous learning pattern about what to do when these new situations surfaced—like when the lights go out.

CHANGING TO DAYLIGHT SAVING TIME

One day while my goddaughters were visiting, Linda, their mom, mentioned several times to make sure I didn't forget to change my clocks for daylight saving time. She knew that repetition really worked for me. Jessie was about three years old at the time, and we noticed she kept moving this little clock of mine around the room. She moved it back and forth from the coffee table to an end table several times. As we watched, she seemed to move it every time her mother said, "Don't forget to change your clocks." We laughed at the sight of this precious child changing or "moving" my clocks for me. How intuitive of this young child to be so helpful and caring. This is one of my favorite "Jessie stories," and I love to remind her about it many times over the years. She has a heart of gold, and throughout my journey, she would create ways to help me learn and heal my brain.

Jessie, who intuitively seemed to know what to do, loved to come up with new games to help stretch my understanding. When I shared some of her ideas with my occupational therapists, they confirmed that she was indeed helping my brain with her inventive games. Jessie would talk to me endlessly on the phone, quizzing me and getting me to think. I didn't have the heart to tell her how painful these conversations and quizzes were for my head. She would always remind me that she was "helping" my brain. I truly believe she is one of the reasons my brain is alive and working today. Pushing and persisting through the pain forced me to keep my brain working, learning, and developing. Due to Jessica's love for me, the pain wasn't as bad as it could have been.

Some Quirky Moments

There have been many quirky moments in my life. I will share some of the ones that stick out in my memory.

While cleaning up after a pizza luncheon at the office, I tried to stuff a square pizza carton into a round garbage hole. I can still picture myself trying to force the carton into the garbage and a coworker staring at me in disbelief. Since my spatial ability had been damaged, this makes sense as to why I couldn't figure it out. But to my coworker, who wasn't aware of my brain injury, she must have thought I was crazy. She finally showed me that I could just fold the box in half and then it would fit into the round hole. I then shared about my brain injury with her.

I found that sharing about my injury and explaining my challenges to others helped to make me feel more comfortable around people. When I hid my disability, it put more pressure on me because I didn't want anyone to see me not able to do something—a major downfall for a perfectionist. Many times I would be afraid to open my mouth for fear I would say something wrong or that I would appear not intelligent, as in the following situation:

One day, during an office party, we were eating cake, and I asked for a spoon instead of a fork. This was a common mistake to get my utensils mixed up. One of my coworkers laughed and sarcastically said, "I think you mean a fork." That hurt.

I know people were not intentionally trying to be mean, but when you have lived your life as a perfectionist and have put high value on your intelligence, comments like this can crush you emotionally. When someone pointed out my mistakes, especially in front of others, it felt like a punch in the face, highlighting for me even more that something was wrong with me. I would be so embarrassed that I said something stupid or incorrect. It also made me face reality that my brain was definitely damaged, even though most of the time I tried so hard to pretend there wasn't anything wrong. I later learned how to laugh off all the hurtful comments.

Another challenge I faced was directions. Many times I didn't know my left from my right. It was worse if I needed to drive or walk somewhere. A couple of times when friends and I were away on vacation and we took the same route each day, they would humorously ask me upon leaving the hotel, "Do we go left or right?" It became almost comical—I would be wrong 100 percent of the time. A friend finally got smart and told me to do the opposite of what I thought. That served me well, especially when I had to take a business trip to Chicago alone and needed to find my way to a restaurant only a few blocks away from my hotel. I remembered my friend's advice who told me to do the opposite of what I thought. By doing this, I would find my way to the restaurant and my way back to the hotel. Sometimes I truly amazed myself that I even ventured out of the house, yet alone go to another city and state. Thankfully cell phones were invented as many times while out alone, someone could be on the phone, just in case I got into a jam. I'm so glad that God gave me a strong spirit of adventure and I didn't live my life in fear.

Two Companies Fighting for One Me

Ten months into my journey, my company of 14 years announced a major transition. They were splitting in two. What are the odds of doing that at the exact time I received my diagnosis of a traumatic brain injury? With this major transition, we would now have to be selected into one of the two companies or let go from the company. Can you imagine? The timing couldn't have been worse!

Many in my organization were unaware of my injury, so leadership decisions were made on my existing skills and performance. Lucky for me, being a top performer to this point in my career served me well. My previous skills and experience would come into play. My immediate bosses felt that given my brain injury and limitations, they would try to keep me with them rather than the new company. Without my knowledge, these conversations took place between my existing leaders and the newly appointed leaders of the spin-off company.

When I first learned of these discussions happening behind my back, it upset me since this meant my bosses were revealing to others about my injury. During this time, I didn't want anyone to know my brain wasn't functioning correctly. This was a personal issue, and it was embarrassing not to be able to perform at the top level. My current bosses felt they could protect me and keep me safe and employed. I learned later that the leaders of the new company felt the same and were willing to take a chance by keeping me on their team even if my brain and high level of performance didn't work the way it did before. Many of these leaders knew me by reputation and were willing to keep me on their team even without knowing how my brain injury journey would end.

What an incredible experience, two companies fighting to keep me employed and on their teams. When I reflect back, without the heightened emotions, I realize how blessed I am to have had so many caring people protecting me during that difficult time in my life.

I'm not sure why, but I did choose the new company and new leadership. Funny how I remember a lot of events and situations but have a lot of blanks as well. I believed the new company would be able to leverage the skills that were still working for me, as well as provide an opportunity for me to stand on my own and not be carried by my existing leaders. While I loved my existing leadership, I didn't want them to have to carry me. I know this is crazy thinking, especially at the most challenging time in my life. But that darn independent personality of mine kicked in. I must have some rebel in my spirit. Many doctors and professional people who work with brain injury survivors tell their patients not to change careers or make any other sudden changes, as it is harder to keep one's life consistent. Regardless, there I went, changing companies, my career and leadership. That is a lot of change for a brain injury person.

The new leaders were very accommodating to any of my limitations. They provided me with a private office instead of a cubicle, limited my working hours to ensure I didn't tire, and kept me in the same working environment where I was familiar with the material and necessary tasks to perform. I would stay at a manager's level, and one of my team members included someone who currently worked for me. This provided consistency in the people I worked with, along with the material and knowledge. Staying at a manager's level enabled me to perform what I did best by leading a team of people and projects versus having to perform detailed and tactical tasks unfamiliar to me.

I stayed with the new company for more than 17 years, including another spin-off followed by a merger. At the time of writing this book, I am still working for the same company. During these years, my job changed many times, which included introducing me to new bosses and new organizations. Each would embrace my limitations caused by the brain injury, as well as value the skills and experiences I didn't lose.

Through my career, I have been given many opportunities to help coworkers learn about my disability. One in particular would play a major role in my healing.

6

Teaching Opportunities

During the years of living with a brain injury, I looked for opportunities to raise awareness about this disability. The first couple of years were challenging and embarrassing. I felt incompetent and thought I appeared dumb to others. As mentioned earlier, it was important for me to be smart and appear smart. Of course, I never considered myself a genius but felt I had an above-average intelligence. Nevertheless, people I knew, and some I didn't know, pointed my mistakes out to me many times when I tried to ask a question, purchase something, or when speaking in general conversation. Not being able to accomplish simple tasks left me feeling really incompetent.

Can you imagine trying to ask someone for a banana and not being able to come up with the word *banana*? I would then try to describe it. It is yellow. You eat it. Sometimes I would be even able to remember it was a fruit. Or when out to dinner with friends, I had to have someone walk with me to the ladies' room because I would get lost trying to find my way back to the table. Well, maybe that one isn't a good example as all ladies typically go to the ladies' room together.

Going out for lunch or dinner and ordering food also proved challenging if I wasn't with someone who could make the selection for me and place my order. I was fortunate to have friends who knew my likes and dislikes regarding food. Menus appeared blurry. All the words came together and seemed to dance around the page, making it almost impossible to read.

Having to use my brain to try to make a food decision was impossible. Trying to narrow my focus, figure out what I liked, and then choose what I wanted to eat were exhausting steps for my brain to process. Now if all I had to do was ask a waiter or waitress for chicken, no problem. But if they asked about sides or additional questions, that's when I would run into trouble.

Those few steps would be a no-brainer to someone without an injury, but, for me, it was an overwhelming, exhausting, frustrating, embarrassing, and impossible task to complete all rolled up into a few minutes. Many times if I knew in advance where we were going to eat, I would check out the menu on the computer in order to be prepared with my selection, and no one in my party would be any wiser. Another trick was to eat at the same type of places and order the same thing every time.

These examples are what the doctors refer to as being a "master" at hiding one's disability. I learned and equipped myself with many tricks to hide and compensate for my limitations so that others wouldn't be aware of how challenging life was for me during my recovery. The ability to disguise my disability was great. The downside? To hide my injury was exhausting and painful to my brain. This caused total fatigue by the end of the day and sometimes lasted a couple of days.

As I became more comfortable living with a brain injury, I used those stumbling moments as opportunities to share with others about what it's like. I can honestly say 100 percent of the people I met knew nothing about a brain injury. Many had never even heard about someone actually injuring their brain. At times, I felt I lived and functioned in a world where I was completely alone and unique—well, at least that is what I thought until about five years into my journey when I met a man and his wife on a cruise.

Imagine! We were assigned the same table for dinner. He had suffered a blow to the head and took medication for seizures. So many times when you hear about other survivors' stories, they seem so much worse than what you are experiencing. Talking with him helped, as finally I could speak with someone who understood what I had been experiencing. I know my friends tried to understand, but until you live with these symptoms and challenges, you just can't truly comprehend. Speaking with this man gave me the push and drive to be able to educate others. Shortly after fully accepting my disability, whenever I would meet someone, within minutes of the conversation, I would tell him or her that I was a brain injury survivor. I would start rattling off statistics by saying, "Did you know that..."

- 5.3 million Americans are living with a brain injury?
- 1.7 million Americans sustain an injury each year?
- Every 21 seconds, someone is diagnosed with an injury?
- There are more people living with a brain injury than any other disease or disability combined?
- And no one is speaking on behalf of these survivors!

This became my message to others. I wanted to be the voice for survivors—those who struggled to speak, those who were still lying in hospital beds, survivors and their families who, like me, were not getting proper medical treatment or else were being misdiagnosed. I believe God gave me this experience so I could raise awareness by telling others, even if only one person at a time.

In time I became aware of a nonprofit group in my home state that was educating and helping survivors. Now I had an organization I could join with to help raise awareness. I became a volunteer to mentor and help other survivors, as well as joined a committee to coordinate an annual fund-raiser walk and raise donations for survivors and their families living in my state.

I have always had a "teaching" spirit, so I finally agreed to write my journey down on paper so I could help others understand what it is like to live with a brain injury. Hopefully, it would give survivors and their families hope and encouragement. I now have an incredible opportunity to teach others about a serious epidemic that is impacting everyone, from the young to seniors, even soldiers fighting to protect our freedom. This injury doesn't discriminate. Anyone can be impacted in an instant. When it happens, lives are changed forever.

HOLISTIC APPROACHES

Many doctors will only use the standard way of healing—drugs, rest, sleep, etc. During my recovery, I chose to listen to the doctors but also listen to my own intuition. I did sleep a lot during the first several years of my recovery but worked very hard not to take all the drugs the doctors were prescribing. The drugs made me very lethargic and foggy. Some made me feel worse than if I had not taken medication. I'm not advocating avoiding taking prescribed medication. I just knew this wasn't the right course for what I was experiencing.

I spent the first three years in a complete fog and often did not understand when someone was talking to me. I can only describe it as having the worst flu of your life. Your head feels like it weighs a ton. Nothing makes any sense. Doctors kept telling me, "You will just need to learn to live with it." I couldn't imagine spending the rest of my life living in this fog. I continued to search for other answers.

One day I happened to attend a holistic event that advertised help for fatigue and pain, etc. The pamphlet described almost everything I was experiencing. After meeting the doctor in attendance and explaining what my life had been like since the accident, he was determined to help me. After just three appointments with this doctor massaging my neck and head, during the middle of one night I awoke to what I believed sounded like a waterfall. I couldn't understand what I was hearing. At that moment, I felt clumps and fluid draining down my throat. The next day, the fog and cloudiness was completely gone, and much of the pressure inside my head had been lifted. I experienced tremendous relief.

Traditional doctors do not want to admit that the work of this doctor, a chiropractor, helped to clear my head. But I know it for sure. Three years prior, every day and moment of my life I lived in a fog with cloudy thinking. Then all of a sudden I had a much clearer head. I believe there was fluid trapped inside my head with no ability to escape. My neck was jammed due to the car accident. With fluid building up around my brain, pressure built up inside my head, as there was no space for the fluid to drain. Amazing how not one of my doctors detected this or had the ability to release the pressure. All I know is, it would be the first of many miracles I would experience living with a brain injury.

MASSAGES AND CRANIOSACRAL THERAPY

I have tried other holistic therapies, such as massages and craniosacral therapy, that have kept my body and brain relaxed, my muscles working and flexible, and kept the pressure off my head. I continue getting a massage at least once a month. Whenever my head and skull are tight and I feel the pressure building up inside my head, I immediately make an appointment for a craniosacral therapy.

Craniosacral therapy is a hands-on method of enhancing the functioning of the membranes and cerebrospinal fluid that surrounds and protects the brain and spinal cord. My head feels so much better after one of these appointments. These therapists are hard to find, and it is important that you ensure you are going to someone who knows what they are doing. While that relieved the pressure in my head, I had daily pain in my head of another kind.

CHIROPRACTORS

For almost ten years, I continued to have daily pain in my head. There were several types.

One type felt like an electrical shock or shooting pains across my whole head, causing me to wince until it was over. It only lasted a few moments but would shoot in all different directions and was quite painful. The second type of pain felt like millions of little pins being stuck throughout my entire head at the same time. The third type of pain can only be described as having my head in a vise and being crushed on both sides of my head. The fourth type of pain felt like someone stabbing my head with a huge knife (like a machete). Depending on what I did during the day, any one of these pains would surface; sometimes I would have them all at the same time. If that happened, the pain was brutal. It was bad enough when I had to manage with one or two of the pains, but when they all hit at the same time, it was almost unbearable. For 13 ½ years, there wasn't one moment when I didn't have one of these type of pains in my head.

During a routine massage, the therapist noticed that my back was out of alignment. She suggested I go to a chiropractor. I made an appointment, and after just a couple of appointments, my back was back in alignment. What happened then could only be described as another of my miracles, as I became aware I wasn't experiencing the intense pain in my head anymore.

When you live with pain every day and then all of a sudden the pain is gone, it is a very strange sensation. I went back to the chiropractor and told him. He wasn't too surprised since he knows how connected the entire body is to the spine and how it connects with the head and brain. It seems amazing that after eight years of going from doctor to doctor about the pain in my head, and the only remedy they knew of was to keep me totally medicated, I finally had some relief from pain in my head—all due to a chiropractor.

Once in a while, if I put in a very long day at the office or am out longer than I should be, the pain and pressure sometimes reappears. But the difference is that now it only takes a day or so to recover, rather than weeks. If I go regularly for routine adjustments, monthly massages, keep my stress level low, eat well and rest, the pain is no longer intense and now tolerable.

The first chiropractor helped to open up my neck to allow the fluid to drain, but he never took x-rays of my neck to learn whether there was even more damage. The second chiropractor focused on the misalignment of my back that ultimately helped my neck and head, but unfortunately he also didn't go further to see there was more damage to my neck. It would take ten years and the tightening of my back muscles after a long plane ride for me to find a third chiropractor who actually listened to my entire story about the car accident and quickly realized no one had ever taken an x-ray of my neck.

Once he did, we found severe whiplash. He carefully worked on my neck area, and it ultimately enabled me to stand up straighter and eliminate a hump at the base of my neck. I've always been skeptical of chiropractors, but I believe there are really good ones out there who look at your body holistically. They focus on what is best for your body and treat the person and the situation by not just jumping in there and cracking (I mean, adjusting) the various areas. I continue to go monthly to my chiropractor and anytime I feel out of sync.

BIOFEEDBACK

One of the other tools I mentioned earlier was biofeedback. This is a technique used that allows your body to provide feedback to you. It helps stroke victims regain movement in paralyzed muscles and helps with relaxation. Sometimes it is even used to help deal with pain. We all use biofeedback in our everyday lives. When we take our temperature with a thermometer, it tells us if we have a fever, or when we jump on a scale, we learn whether we have gained or lost weight. These are all forms of biofeedback. Our bodies feed information back to us and help us to take action. It might be to get rest and drink plenty of fluids or to stop eating those ice cream sundaes and lose weight.

A nurse worked with me to learn biofeedback techniques. She would hook me up to a machine (just a couple of wires on my fingers and skull) that would read back to me when I was overexercising my brain or when my body and muscles became too tightly clenched. By using this machine, it helped me to retrain myself to relax my muscles and brain. This would then take the pressure off my head and skull. She explained to me that if I had a broken leg, it would have been put in a cast, and I would have to stay off my leg for a period of time. The same thing applied to my brain. But how do you stop your brain from functioning or give it a rest?

The brain controls everything you do—breathing, thinking, moving, etc. Twice a day, I listened to a tape that taught me to relax, which stopped my brain from becoming too focused. This was challenging for me since my brain was always thinking, even when sleeping. These techniques made me aware of when my body and muscles tightened or my brain became too focused.

While sitting, I had a habit of crossing one leg over the other and wildly swinging it back and forth—most of it done unconsciously. You could easily say my body continued to be in constant motion. I just couldn't sit still. After learning these techniques I quickly recognized when my legs were swinging, thus enabling me to break the habit. I could also tell when I became anxious or tightened up my muscles. I even noticed that my speech became slower, and I didn't talk as fast as I did in the past. One of my coworkers even commented on how calm I appeared even when a crisis arose at work. Staying calm in these situations allowed my brain to process the information better and not become caught up in the craziness at work. I could calmly look at the situation and react. I really believe in learning biofeedback techniques and recommend them to any brain injury survivor or anyone who needs to build relaxation into their daily life.

EYE SPECIALISTS

For many years, I had pain in, around, and behind my eyes. Since I've worn both contacts and glasses for most of my adult life, I routinely went for eye exams. My eye doctor was well aware of my brain injury and always did certain tests to ensure that my eyes were all right. But nothing could ever be done for the eye pain. A friend, while surfing the web looking for help for me, found an eye doctor who specializes in brain injury patients. What a difference it made for my eyes to have someone who understood how the brain and eyes are connected.

He did many tests to ensure I saw correctly and that the messages were getting to my brain in a timely fashion but found a big delay from the time I saw something until the time it took that information to reach my brain. How amazing he could identify a gap through a simple test. It now made sense. My brain was working overtime to try and process what my eyes were seeing. The overexertion of my brain caused the pain in both my eyes and head. Thankfully, each year we would see improvement and a decrease in the delay time as well as the pain in my eyes. I continued to rest my eyes to avoid eyestrain, and it helped to manage the pain. It continues to amaze me how much our entire bodies are connected to our brains and how the parts of the body work together. When one part isn't working properly, it impacts the rest.

As I started to see improvements in working with different specialists and new techniques, I became determined to continue to learn and identify new opportunities to help strengthen my brain and body and to create effective solutions to tackle everyday situations. I knew I was on my own and needed to find the answers myself, as there didn't seem to be a road map for this journey.

Where would my new journey take me? Could I find creative solutions to help me live in mainstream society and ultimately help other survivors?

7

Things That Helped

There are many organizations, as well as people, that can help brain injury survivors. Unfortunately, I was totally unaware of them in the early years of my disability. Therefore, my journey took me to many places, causing me to try countless new ideas. Some of these occurred early in my journey while others I found much later. Here are a few opportunities I've leveraged.

PHYSICAL THERAPY

I met my first physical therapist more than ten months into my journey. Physical therapy helped my body to start moving again after not doing anything for almost a year. My physical therapists guided and instructed me into using my muscles again, making sure they didn't put too much pressure on my brain so as not to cause any pain in my head. Pain in my head? You don't realize when you are exerting the muscles in your legs or arms that you are also exerting your brain. I found out very quickly that any movement of my legs or arms caused intense pressure on my brain and head. Therefore, we took this journey very slow and easy.

In physical therapy, I learned I could no longer do two activities simultaneously—like tossing a ball and talking at the same time. One of my exercises consisted of standing and walking on a balance beam on the floor. As a former gymnast, I felt that this should be easy—or so I thought. All I needed to do was toss a weighted ball back and forth to another patient, a young man, while balancing on the beam. As we tossed the ball, he commented to the other therapists, "This isn't fair. She's not having any trouble while I keep falling off the beam." When trying to catch or throw the ball, he couldn't keep his balance and would fall off the beam. I, on the other hand, seemed to be doing fine. After his comment, the therapist said, "Just watch this." She began having a conversation with me. I immediately fell off the beam. Amazing! I couldn't focus on the conversation and toss a ball to someone at the same time.

So that began a new therapy routine for me—trying to do two things at the same time. I had to walk the halls of the hospital holding on to a bar on the side of the wall while having a conversation with the therapist. For me, this felt harder than someone trying to walk with a sprained ankle or jog on a treadmill. It felt like an impossible task and at the same time scary and emotionally sad that something so simple could be so challenging, overwhelming, and painful. Ultimately, I graduated to walking and talking without holding the bar attached to the wall and feeling less pain. Several times before therapy, I had fallen down stairs, all because I tried talking to someone at the same time. This is why most times taking an elevator became an easier choice. Imagine…talking and holding a conversation turned out to be just as challenging as walking.

Emotionally, it was hard to go to physical therapy. Why? Because to many I looked perfectly normal, while others in the waiting room were in wheelchairs or on crutches. Some had casts removed—something to at least show there was something wrong—while I stood there feeling so out of sorts and lost. One time while on a treadmill and only able to walk 0.8 miles per hour, an elderly gentleman (who looked old enough to be my grandfather) next to me appeared to be practically running. So many times I wanted to shout out, "I have a brain injury, and this is as fast as I can go!" These types of emotions screamed inside of me throughout the years.

While therapy was hard both physically and mentally, it did help me tremendously in my recovery. I'm so glad the therapists were all nice and helpful.

PERSONAL TRAINER

Working with a personal trainer helped my muscles and body grow stronger. Of course, this was years after the accident and physical therapy. A personal trainer can also help customize endurance programs to help strengthen your body. My trainer taught me how to use exercise equipment and guided my progress. Being an overachiever, I had a tendency to overwork my body, which caused pain in my brain and added to my exhaustion. Working with the trainer enabled me to pace my exercises without causing further pain and fatigue. Building up my endurance and increasing my body strength enabled me to do more without experiencing any pain. It also reduced my fatigue; therefore, I didn't need to nap as often.

OCCUPATIONAL THERAPY

I didn't receive formal occupational therapy until many years into my journey. I found these therapists helpful in sorting out strategies to help compensate for the areas of my brain that weren't performing like they did before the injury. They revealed to me that I intuitively had already come up with many strategies on my own that were helping my brain. However, they helped me figure out which activities tired me out and which didn't. I learned to do the tiring activities when I had lots of energy and save the less tiring activities for when I was more fatigued. This awareness made me become more aware of when fatigue hit me. It warned me not to even try to tackle something challenging as it would only leave me frustrated and feeling as if I failed at something. This served me well in my years living with this disability.

Physical and occupational therapy are great; however, many insurance companies only allow so many visits, so, for me, I had several sessions and then had to be sent back out into the world to figure out the rest on my own. I'm so blessed that I have a tenacious attitude that enabled me to fight my way through this disability. I continued to seek out other ways to strengthen my body and brain. Personal trainers, the computer, and kid games compensated for what I would have received if I had been able to stay with the physical and occupational therapy sessions.

Here is what I found that helped make my journey easier.

PERSONAL SHOPPER

Clothes shopping in a store can be difficult and challenging. When walking into a store, my brain became completely overwhelmed, causing dizziness, confusion, and complete exhaustion. It felt like the circuits in my brain were completely in overload, firing out of control and then shutting down, making it difficult for me to walk through a store and identify what I needed. Further, the lights in the stores, the hustle and bustle of people, the music playing over the loudspeakers, etc., can all drastically impact a brain injury survivor, causing disorientation, pain, and confusion. Add all that to the physical act of trying something on. I can't tell you how many times I walked into a store, circled the store perimeters, and then walked back out with nothing to show except pain and exhaustion. Then home for a nap.

Having someone who either knows your style or can learn your style of clothes and then do all the hard work at selecting the outfits for you is very helpful. I have used a personal shopper in the store to make my selections for me while I sat waiting in the dressing room.

After she selected different styles based on my preference, all I had to do was try them on in a quiet, secluded room and the personal shopper would tell me what looked good. Many shopping malls provide the personal shoppers service for free.

I have also been blessed with friends and family who did my clothes shopping for me. While out shopping for themselves, if they saw something they thought I might like, they picked it up—anything from jewelry to work clothes to household needs. This has been a lifesaver for me

CLEANING PERSON

Having someone to come in to clean my house at least once a month is extremely helpful. By the time the weekend came, after putting in a long week at the office, pushing a vacuum cleaner added more pressure to my head. The person I hired did the heavy cleaning, relieving me of doing those chores and enabling me to not get tired. I feel a little spoiled and lazy but have found this to be an incredible aid in helping to make my life easier. Paying someone to help with these activities saves me energy, thus facilitating time for me to spend with my goddaughters, friends, and family. It is worth the expense.

SOMEONE TO DRIVE

As I mentioned earlier, driving was challenging and completely drained my energy. The ability to stay focused on the road and not be distracted by the radio or someone talking in the car, even spotting an animal outside the car window, takes so much brain power. It increases fatigue and ultimately brings on that exhausted feeling. Having someone drive me provided me with the opportunity to do more, especially if we were going to a party or event. I could attend and, if I got overtired, not worry about having to drive home. Not being able to drive made me lose some of my independence, but I gained the energy to spend more time with family and friends and get back into the world. I have now become very comfortable with others driving, and I just automatically jump into the passenger seat.

EARPLUGS

Earplugs are great at blocking out some of the sounds that contribute to the vibration that rattles inside my head. I carry a pair of earplugs with me at all times. I've used them at plays when the music or speakers are too loud and at work when conversations are too distracting. They've even come in handy at the airport while waiting to board a plane, when people are talking all around me and overhead speakers are just too much for my head and brain to take. They have been especially helpful in New York City, where horns continuously blow, fire trucks fly past, and the hustle and bustle of traffic create noise and vibrations that are just too much for my brain to handle. Earplugs have been an essential piece of equipment that I never leave home without.

QUIET WORKSPACE

Throughout my career, I have been fortunate to have managers and leaders who provided me with whatever I needed. Many companies today have turned offices into cubicles versus private offices. Prior to my brain injury, I loved working in cubicles. My team sat all around me, which made it fun to shout out answers to someone's question or just listen to how they handled situations or what they did over the weekend. We all had a great working relationship. At times, you could hear people telling jokes and just enjoying each other's company. Being a focused individual, I could block out any type of distraction when I needed to. However, after the accident, it was a different story. I couldn't block out any noise or conversations.

In the beginning of my recovery, I still stayed in my cubicle surrounded by my coworkers, but because I was still in a fog at that stage, the noise didn't distract me too much—or so I thought. However, as I began to lose the fogginess and my brain began to slowly wake up, the noise around me grew louder and louder inside my head. It became increasingly difficult to try and focus or concentrate on something. The harder my brain had to work, the more energy I lost. I grew extremely tired. One of the occupational therapists suggested I work in a quiet space where it would cut down on the distraction and noise. My boss accommodated this request and moved me immediately into a private office, which helped tremendously.

The people I've worked with over the years have been great, and nobody ever made a fuss with me having an office while they sat in a cubicle. I tried many times to go back out into the cubicle environment as I missed working next to my coworkers, but each time my headaches and tiredness increased, causing trouble in focusing and concentrating. Just that little request to my management made a major impact on my life. It gave me the ability to do my job more effectively as well as give me a better quality of life.

MEETING OTHERS AT SUPPORT GROUPS

Meeting other brain injury survivors is a great experience. For many years, I felt to be the only one living with this disability. Everyone around me never heard of a brain injury and never knew anyone living with one. I felt completely different from everyone else. After attending some support groups, it awakened me to the realization there were others just like me. How validating when others nodded their heads in agreement when symptoms and experiences were discussed! It really helped to be able to relate my experiences with others and also discuss and share what I've learned to make the journeys of others easier.

Experienced brain injury survivors and their families can help pave the way and provide helpful hints as to what the journey involves for survivors and their families who are new to this world. Most of the support groups I've attended are made up of survivors, family members, and professionals in the brain injury community, all of which provide a great resource. They've been through this journey before and can provide advice or an empathetic ear with a better understanding than friends and family. While my friends and family tried, it wasn't until I met other survivors and professionals that many of my questions got addressed and answered.

DAILY PLANNER

After the accident, as I've mentioned before, I became easily confused and disorganized. Can you imagine being escorted to your desk, sitting down, and seeing a flashing light on your telephone and not having a clue what it meant? My team members had to show me how to retrieve voice messages. Even after listening to the message, I didn't understand what the person said or if I needed to take action or respond. While having lunch with a consultant friend, I explained my situation to him. He suggested I get a daily planner, which would help me organize my thoughts and record phone messages. He ended up buying me my own daily planner and coaching me on how to use it, how to listen to the message and write it down in my planner. What a great gift! This helped so much, and I continue to use a planner today. I keep all my important phone numbers and key facts in it and record all my activities and tasks I need to do either personally or professionally. I never leave home without it. It even feels great to cross off my tasks when I've completed them. It gives me a great feeling of accomplishment.

GIVING YOURSELF A BREAK

Many brain injury survivors want to live their lives exactly as they did prior to their injury; however, life has now changed. This has to be acknowledged. The challenge is learning how to recognize what we are able to do and what we are not able to do. I decided to focus on what came natural for me.

The type of work I did for a living continued to come naturally, such as coaching and managing people. It also included washing clothes, sorting the mail, and doing household errands. So I focused on the activities that came naturally for me, and it enabled me to realize how much I could still accomplish. My biggest struggle had to do with numbers, money, and finances. I recognized this as a problem area and searched for others who could help me with these activities. I also found ways to work around these activities, like not balancing my checkbook and keeping enough money in my account to ensure I didn't bounce a check. I hired a financial planner to handle my finances. He is naturally aware of my situation and takes the time to help me understand the financial information I can't understand. He has my best interest at heart, and I trust him.

It is also important to recognize when to do certain activities. For example, I only run errands on the weekend since I know driving to stores tires me out. I learned to go out in the morning to tackle errands and then to nap in the afternoon to recover. Doing the laundry does not take a lot of energy out of me, so I typically put a load of wash in after work on Thursdays or Fridays. Doing the laundry after getting home from work and before retiring for the evening enabled me to cross off one more activity on my to-do list without exerting too much energy or experiencing pain. The harder tasks, like changing the bedsheets or paying the bills, had to be done on a Sunday afternoon when I had more energy. Recognizing what takes up your energy and what doesn't has been a great resource for me. I prioritize my days and my weeks so that I can leverage as much energy as possible for what's important to me.

It is important to give yourself a break. I try very hard not to get upset if I don't get all my to-dos finished for the week or the day. When I get down because I can't accomplish something or get frustrated when I have to rest after doing something, I try hard to remember all my accomplishments after the accident that early in my recovery caused limitations. It is important to recognize how far you've come. This can be done by writing down your accomplishments and keeping them as a reference to remind yourself how much improvement you've made over time.

TAKING NOTES

I am now a firm believer in writing everything down and not relying on memory. Prior to my injury, I didn't take notes at all. I had a photographic memory and could remember dates, times, places, events, and even where people were sitting in an office meeting when decisions were made. Amazing how much could be crammed into my brain. At work, coworkers would ask me their questions instead of looking up the information. As their resource library, I didn't realize what a gift I had until I lost it. After the accident, it became important to write down everything in my day planner. When someone asked Albert Einstein for his phone number, he had to look it up. When questioned, he said, "Why should I memorize something I can so easily get from a book." He supported the idea that we should not clutter our brains with meaningless details when it is easy enough to look up the information. This comforted me when I realized I could do the same by writing something down and then giving myself permission to refer to my notes, or looking something up versus having to use my brain to try and remember—all of which would have put more stress and strain on my brain. I learned to always carry a notepad and pencil or pen with me, whether it is for something personal or professional. I never wanted to be caught off guard if someone asked me to do something and I had to rely on my memory. Writing myself notes takes the pressure off in trying to remember everything. It also gives me an opportunity to cross off the items when completed, something I love to do. I guess that is why I haven't purchased an electronic organizer; it is more fun for me to cross off the activities I do rather than pressing a delete button.

Writing something down gives the appearance of having a better memory. Many friends and coworkers comment on what a great memory I have, and it is all because I take notes and jot everything down. Writing down tasks and keeping notes frees up your brain to focus on other things—things that you feel are more important.

MEMORY GAMES

Many times I try to balance keeping my brain active without tiring it out. Every day I try to tackle the TV guide crossword puzzle. This is a great activity for everyone's brain. Art Linkletter, a Canadian-born American radio and television personality, who died at the age of 97, had very sharp cognitive skills and memory right up to his death. He credited keeping his brain sharp by doing crossword puzzles. For example, when reading crossword puzzle questions down or across, you use one part of your brain. When thinking of the answer, you use another part of your brain. Then by writing down the answer, another part of your brain gets exercised.

Amazing, isn't it? In the past, these puzzles were so easy to complete. At the height of my injury, I could only tackle one question before needing to stop and rest my eyes and brain. It would take hours later, or sometimes not until another day, before I could try to tackle the next question. Attempting to complete just one crossword puzzle might take me days or maybe even weeks. Unfortunately, many times I never even finished the crossword puzzle. I discovered, as a brain injury survivor, that I was great at starting a task but rarely finished it. Not finishing became a hard reality to handle since my normal mode of operating always included finishing anything I started, even if challenging.

I have also been fortunate to have the presence of young children in my life during the time of my recovery. The games they played, such as Concentration, Scattergories, or matching or memory games, were great at helping to stimulate my memory. It is fun playing with children because they don't realize you have anything wrong with your brain. And if they win, people just naturally assume you let them win.

There are also great games you can play on the computer. I found playing Solitaire, FreeCell, Spider, and other card games also helped my brain grow. It became easy to tell when my brain was tiring because while certain games could be easily won, when tired and my brain wasn't functioning properly, they were difficult to complete. I used these games as a benchmark in my progress. When I began playing them, I struggled; nevertheless, I was able to measure my progress by the number of times I won. As the games started to get easier, I realized how much my brain had healed.

BEGIN SLOWLY

It is important not to take on the world once you begin feeling better. I noticed that when I started to run errands for myself, I would tend to overdo it. I had to recognize that being out for half an hour was long enough. Then I slowly worked up to being out for a couple of hours. It is important to stretch yourself so that you are growing and stimulating your brain, but at the same time, you need to keep a realistic pace so you don't get overly fatigued and reinjure the areas of your brain that had been damaged. This proved challenging for me. When I started to feel strong, I wanted to make up for lost time and do everything I could think of doing. Taking it easy with baby steps became the mission I had to set for many years.

NUTRITION

Proper nutrition is also important and beneficial for brain injury survivors. I noticed if I missed a meal or didn't get enough protein, I became tired and weak. I could tell by how sluggish my brain reacted. My words also became more tangled and confused. My friends noticed how quickly I began to fade right before it was time for me to have lunch or dinner.

There are many foods that are great for your brain, such as salmon and foods containing omega-3. The hard part for me is that I don't like a lot of the foods that are beneficial for my brain, but I'm now learning to eat healthier. Drinking lots of water has also been helpful. My doctor wrote a referral to allow me to work with a nutritionist during my journey, and the insurance company paid for it. This provided another opportunity to leverage in my journey to get back into "mainstream society."

As you can see, it took a long time to research and find the appropriate resources, people, and organizations to help me in my journey. Each step has been worth it as I continued to improve and get stronger and healthier, all of which has enabled me to have a better quality of life and get back into mainstream society.

Since most of this journey has been both what I remember or have documented along the way, I asked a couple of friends to share their recollections. What they recalled amazed and humbled me.

8

Friends' Observations

As you can imagine from what I've already described from notes I took along the way, my memory and recollection of the first couple of years is not the best. However, friends and coworkers shared their observations of me before, during, and after my recovery. Therefore, I asked them to write them down.

Marlene is a friend I met at work. She moved to New Mexico in 1993 (before the accident), and we continued to stay in touch by telephone. Here are her thoughts:

> "I worked closely with Donna at AT&T Corporate Headquarters from '89–'93. She was always extremely busy and very dedicated to her job. She didn't mind being a workaholic. I always had to remind her to take a break or to eat lunch. She said that she couldn't wait for the day that all a human would have to do is take a pill every morning and not have to ever eat.
>
> "Donna came to NM in '97... a couple of years after her accident. I was so happy to see her and to be able to spend some time with her. However,

she wasn't the same vivacious, confident, energetic, comical, take-charge person I once knew. Even her eyes were not the same beautiful, clear, baby blue I had always admired.

"It seemed as if she was in a daze and hardly realized she was on vacation. It didn't matter to her what was on the agenda, I could tell that she was just going through the motions and didn't enjoy her trip at all.

"I was able to see the 'before' and the 'after,' and there was definitely a huge difference in her personality, her emotions, her thoughts, and her actions. A brain injury is a devastating condition to endure, and I'm thrilled that after all these years have gone by, Donna is finally the same Donna I once knew. Welcome back, Donna!"

Betsy is a friend who I worked with closely at the time of my accident and who never seemed to leave my side throughout my incredible journey. To this day, we are still friends and have stayed in touch even though we are no longer working together.

"Donna, you continue to be an inspiration to us all for your resiliency, determination, ability to continually perform under the worst circumstances, and always being grateful for the help we all felt compelled to offer you. Here are some things I remember about that time:

- *Never leaving your side when we went to meetings*
- *Making sure you got and ate your lunch*
- *Watching out for you when we traveled*
- *Helping you finish your sentences when you stumbled*
- *Providing a safe place to "fall/vent" when someone was unsympathetic to what you were*

experiencing or when someone in the organization was driving us all crazy

• *Insisting you sleep over at my house when we came back from a work event in New York City, thus enabling you not to have to drive and so I could also take care of you after such a long work event.*

• *Always amazed at what you were able to accomplish even though you were pretty much always in pain"*

Dawn is a former boss and now a great friend. Dawn and I made an instant lifelong connection. She has been an incredible supporter of my injury as a boss and now a friend.

"In 2005, I had the fortunate opportunity to hire Donna on my new team to support Organizational Change Management (OCM) for the major IT delivery programs across the organization. Since this was a new team for a new 'organization-wide' initiative, I lead the team through several brainstorming exercises to gather ideas & suggestions about our team structure, objectives, priorities, and major deliverables. I knew of Donna's brain injury and was always very conscious of managing her time during these brainstorming exercises, which at times even made the 'non-brain injured' employees tired and wornout. She always had great ideas, so I was careful not to over-do it and I made sure she had appropriate 'downtime' or assigned her more passive work tasks in between harder tasks.

"With appropriate time management, Donna's flow or ideas was like a water fountain... they just kept coming. Many of them were successfully implemented and operationalized across many of the programs. Across the team and the leadership, Donna

was considered a 'thought-leader' and was depended upon for generating 'out of the box' ideas that others could not do as well. We capitalized on what she could do and worked around the areas where she struggled.

"In the office, I remember supporting Donna in moving into a single private office space with walls/closed door, to help reduce the amount of noise and distractions around her. This made a big difference in her productivity and overall health while at work.

"As a manager of a brain injury survivor it was rewarding to be able to support Donna and at the same time leverage the skills and talents she was capable of while working at her own pace and in a safe environment. Donna was one of my highest performers on the team, always delivered on her accomplishments and was highly respected by her peers and leadership team.

"Many were not aware of Donna's disability and felt threatened by her competitively when it came to performance reviews. They were respectful of and to Donna, while viewing her as the "person to beat." As her manager, I was glad to be able protect her enough so she could remain as an outstanding member of my team."

9

My Healing Moment

While living through my brain injury journey, my thinking and belief was that God had purposely prepared and called me to live as a brain injury survivor. Why? So I could help make an impact on others with the same disability.

As I went from doctor to doctor, from hospital to rehabilitation center, I met many survivors and their families and shared my journey of hope with them. It felt so good to be able to tell them my life experiences and stories of being able to work and that I could thrive and survive as a brain injury survivor. What an awesome feeling and experience to see hope on their faces even while they were still in therapy struggling with their symptoms and limitations. I'm humbled to think I could be used by God to accomplish this.

Many survivors shared in their own way about how my stories had helped them. I will never forget one young man's face as he beamed with hope and excitement as I shared my experiences to a group at a rehabilitation center. At the end of my talk, this young man couldn't get to the front of the room fast enough to ask me for a hug. That's all he wanted—a simple hug. I left even more inspired and humbled to know that even though my own journey had been challenging, it appeared totally worth it at that moment—especially after the hug and smile from the young man who now had hope and believed he could get better all because I shared my incredible journey.

Another experience I remember so clearly is a woman who had been struggling with her injury, but I didn't learn how much my story impacted her life until years later when I met this woman and her husband at a brain injury conference. Her husband shared with me that after his wife attended a session where I spoke, she told her husband, "One day I want to do what Donna is doing." My story gave her encouragement and the belief she would also be able to share her story with others. She and her husband are doing well and have trained their dogs so they can take them to hospitals to meet other survivors. What an incredible experience to know God used someone like me to impact the life of this woman, and now she is impacting the lives of many others. But there's more.

My biggest experience would come 13 ½ years after my accident when I learned that ultimately God's plan for me was to be completely healed of my brain injury.

In May 2008, a coworker friend invited me to attend a Women's Conference at her church. I knew the day might be challenging as there were many women in attendance, and I anticipated a lot of noise, music, and distractions. Nevertheless, for some reason, I said yes. Elisa was well aware of my injury and limitations, so I knew I would be in good hands. I don't remember much of the day except for a couple of significant events.

Significant event number 1. We had to choose which conference session to attend. The sessions were identified by Bible scriptures and nothing else. No additional details. Not being a Bible expert, I only knew one of the listed scriptures on the schedule—Mark 5:34, the story of a woman who had an issue with blood and who was healed after 12 years when she touched the hem of Jesus's garment. During my journey, for some reason, that scripture resonated with me. I would think about it and read it often. Jesus said, "Daughter, your faith has made you well." I believed strongly that one day I would hear God saying those exact words to me. Each morning of the 13 ½ years living with my brain injury, I would awake believing this was the day I would be totally free of the symptoms while at the same time believing God had called me to live as a brain injury survivor. As you can see, I had some conflicting thoughts. Since Mark 5:34 had a special place in my heart and the only scripture at this time I was familiar with, we decided to attend that session.

I don't remember anything the speaker said, but that didn't matter because Elisa heard every word. Halfway through the session, my friend would leap up from her chair in the middle of the speaker's talk and say to me, "Did you hear that? Did you hear that?" She became so excited and animated. The speaker had been sharing about God's healing power. Of course, I didn't hear it, so I wasn't sure what she was all excited about. At the end of the session, she told me I could be healed of the brain injury and wanted me to meet the speaker. At lunchtime, we caught up with the speaker, and my friend told her about my brain injury.

Significant event number 2. The speaker, Cathy confirmed what Elisa believed to be true. She said that I could be healed of the brain injury. Now of course I looked at her as if she was crazy. I had test scores, records, and MRI scans as living proof of the damage to my brain.

I can't recall every single thing Cathy shared with us, but she did leave a big impression and one comment that lingered in my mind, "You identify yourself as a brain injury survivor." My initial thought? Of course I did, and I was proud to be a survivor. Months later I would recognize this would be the key to unlocking my healing.

After the conference, I continued to mull over Cathy's comment and also started to attend my friend's church. There I had the opportunity to meet with Cathy who attended the same church. She continued to share scriptures from the Bible on healing. I wrote them down, read them all the time, many times speaking them out loud so I could hear them.

However, my mind was conflicted. I read all the scriptures in the Bible on healing and believed I could be healed, but at the same time, I kept holding on to my brain injury, proud to be a survivor. Since I thought God had given me this as a gift so I could help others, I had trouble believing I could be totally healed of every symptom. I didn't realize I needed to reprogram my thinking about healing.

Several months later, I took a firm stand for what I now believe about healing. I decided to remove the green bracelet I had been wearing to market and raise awareness about brain injuries. I also made a decision to park my car at work where everyone else parked. As I mentioned earlier, the employee parking lot was rather large, necessitating a long walk to and from the car, and I also had that incline to deal with.

I was determined to "walk by faith" and believe I was healed of the brain injury, even though I still had challenging symptoms. I wanted to demonstrate my faith and understanding of God's Word I had been reading in the Bible and heard preached at church. So on the appointed day, I removed the "handicap" sticker from my car window and parked my car in the large lot behind my office building. I took the long walk (well, to me it was a long walk) to the office, worked all day, and then challenged myself to make the incline back to the parking lot. Out of breath, slowly moving up the incline, I made it to the top and actually found my car.

The following Sunday, after removing my green bracelet and removing the handicap parking sticker from my car, my life changed dramatically again. At the end of the church service, a worship leader prayed for the manifestation of my healing. By then, in my mind and heart, I knew I was healed even though I still lived with symptoms. My same friend, who was convinced I would be healed, was with me as the worship leader prayed, and she saw in her mind an egg timer go *ding*—like time is up. I wasn't sure what to think when she shared that image with me. Yet I would learn that very day what the egg timer meant.

I drove home from church. I'm not sure I can explain or articulate what happened, but all of a sudden, the pain in my head that I had been living with 24/7 and for 13 ½ years disappeared in an instant. It felt like a cloud lifted from my head and was being pulled toward the sky. I could feel it. Also at that moment, I understood the scriptures I had been studying and praying about. They suddenly came alive to me and became real. My mind-set changed, and instead of holding on to the brain injury as a gift from God, the true gift was to be healed from the brain injury. All I can say is that I knew, that I knew, that I knew, I was healed. When you live with pain for so many years, you know for sure when it leaves you for good. My mind and brain were finally awake from a very long sleep, now alert and ready to begin another new journey.

What an incredible experience—first living with the brain injury and then being totally healed. I'm not sure why God chose me for this journey, but I do know that God is not a respecter of persons, and if He can do it for me, He can do it for anyone. I don't know what your journey will entail, but God's healing ability and love for us is immeasurable. God has blessed me with a new journey to not only share what it has been like to live with a brain injury but to pass on my story of healing to others.

10

Rainbows

I believe there are reasons for everything that happens in our lives. I know the challenges I have faced growing up prepared me for this experience. How do you explain a shy, quiet girl who, throughout her school years and at the beginning of her working career, would now be able to speak publicly to groups of brain injury survivors? Fortunately, as my working career progressed, I was given opportunities to participate in public speaking events. They prepared me by giving me the confidence I needed to speak in front of others. Now I can use this skill to speak to other survivors about my experience and help give them hope and encouragement.

I also work as a mentor to brain injury survivors. As a "people manager" for a large company, I've been able to develop the skills acquired there as coach and mentor, providing me with the opportunity to speak on a one-to-one basis with individuals, provide coaching tips, and offer advice about strategies I learned over the years. Just being able to listen to other survivors and having them know that I understand what they are experiencing is so comforting. It has also proved a blessing to their families. It is rewarding to be able to use the gifts God has given me, as well as the experience of living with a brain injury, so that I can have an impact and make a difference in their lives.

Unfortunately, I didn't have the opportunity to meet other survivors during the early years of my recovery. I believe this would have helped me to have a mentor, someone to talk with who truly understood what I was going through and help coach me along the way. Yes, friends and family always tried to say the right things, but many times they frustrated me even more because they just didn't understand what I was feeling or experiencing. Now I'm using the skills that I have learned to help others.

It is important to keep a positive attitude, set goals, and continue to work towards getting better. I have listed some skills on strategies and time management in the appendix.

I believe there is a voice built inside each of us that guides us in our many journeys. It is one of the many rainbows that God uses to enhance our life. Listening to doctors is important, but listening to your own inner voice is much more important. The key is to listen to the voice and work toward achieving your goals.

Recognize the rainbows in your life. I have been truly blessed with many, such as having great people in my life, many who came into my life after the brain injury. And just as I search the sky for a rainbow after it has rained, each day I look for a new rainbow—a new goal to tackle, something to accomplish that I couldn't do before, or someone new to share my incredible journey with.

Rainbows have always played a significant role in my life. Through them, I continue to learn so much about myself. They would appear during the most difficult times in my life, and when I saw one, I knew God was right beside me assuring me everything would be all right. Rainbows are God's way of showing His mercy and His promise, and I know that more will be provided as I seek ways to use the gifts and talents God has given me to help other brain injury survivors

I pray each day that you will find your rainbows too.

APPENDIX

Here are some strategies and time management tips I've learned from occupational therapists that I used frequently throughout my journey and still do.

TEN STRATEGIES

1. Know your attention limitations and take a break when necessary. Set your watch or a timer to remind yourself to rest.
2. Determine the times of day when you are most attentive and have the most energy and complete the most demanding tasks during those times.
3. Be sure to get enough sleep on a consistent basis as fatigue will further reduce attention capabilities.
4. Arrange your work environment to minimize visual distractions and use earplugs or headphones to reduce noisy distractions.
5. Take rest periods when changing tasks. This enables time to adjust to something new.
6. Write down things that you want to remember immediately (carry pads, Post-it notes, day planners with you). Or if out of the office or house, call yourself and leave a message on your answering machine.
7. Use electronic devices (pagers, telephone dialers with preprogrammed numbers, voice-activated telephone dialing, calculators, tape recorders, key finders, answering machines, laptop computers, car finders)
8. Keep items such as keys, purse, wallet, etc., in the same places.
9. Slow down and take time while reading. If necessary, read things more than once. Doing so will help you process the information. Do the same when writing and speaking.
10. Ask people to talk slowly or ask them to repeat what they've said. This will help give you time to process what is being said.

TEN TIPS FOR TIME MANAGEMENT

1. Make a list, prioritize, and check things off as you get them done. Write out goals for the day, week, and month; include work, home, and school.
2. Review your list from time to time. Is everything on the list necessary?
3. Ask yourself, "What is the best use of my time right now?" Then do it!
4. Be willing to sacrifice "perfection" to get things done.
5. Learn to say no to demands that don't benefit you.
6. Whenever possible, delegate!
7. Don't waste time on minor decisions.
8. Arrange your work time to keep interruptions to a minimum.
9. Be realistic about what you can accomplish during a given period.
10. Plan your work for those times when your energy is at its peak and use your less energetic times for leisure or for a nap.

I hope what I've learned over the years and shared will benefit brain injury survivors and their families. I believe I lived through this journey for a reason, and if I can help others by what I've experienced, it will have been a journey worth taking.

ABOUT THE AUTHOR

Donna has always wanted to help people even as a young girl grow-ing up in New Jersey. In her early years, she donated to charities to support others with disabilities and life-changing experiences. As she grew up, she volunteered in the community and participated in numerous charitable walks. Never would she believe that one day, her coworkers, friends, and family would be walking and raising money for her.

In 1995, Donna's world changed when she sustained a trau-matic brain injury. After many years of occupational, physical, and cognitive therapy, along with holistic approaches and her faith, Donna began her long journey toward recovery.

Donna's goal is to raise awareness through her story of faith and recovery. She also mentors brain injury survivors, along with their family members, by sharing her journey and what it was like to live with a brain injury. Donna wasn't given much hope after her diagno-sis; however, her story is inspiring and an encouragement to others that nothing is impossible, especially with God on their side.

CPSIA information can be obtained
at www.ICGtesting.com
Printed in the USA
BVHW031325060121
597153BV00006B/75